Leigh Weimers'
Guide to Silicon Valley

Leigh Weimers' Guide to Silicon Valley
An Insider's Tips for Techies and Tourists

By
Leigh Weimers

To John — Enjoy the Valley! Leigh Weimers — 1994

Western Tanager Press
Santa Cruz, Ca 95060

Edited by Susan Hurley
Cover Art by Nina Paley
Cover Design by Lynn Piquett
Text Design by Susan Hurley
Maps by Maggie Leighly
Typography by TypaGraphix

ISBN: 0-934136-52-1

Library of Congress Card Catalog Number: 93-060450

Printed in the United States of America

Western Tanager Press
1111 Pacific Avenue
Santa Cruz, CA 95060

Acknowledgements

The author wishes to thank Clyde Arbuckle, *The Business Journal,* Yvette del Prado, Joseph Izzo Jr., *Metro,* Michael S. Malone, Marjorie Pierce, David Plotnikoff, San Jose Convention and Visitors Bureau, San Jose Historical Museum, San Jose Metropolitan Chamber of Commerce, *San Jose Mercury News,* San Jose Real Estate Board and Paul Tumason, without whose assistance this book could not have been written, and Geri Weimers, without whose patience and encouragement this writing would not have been possible.

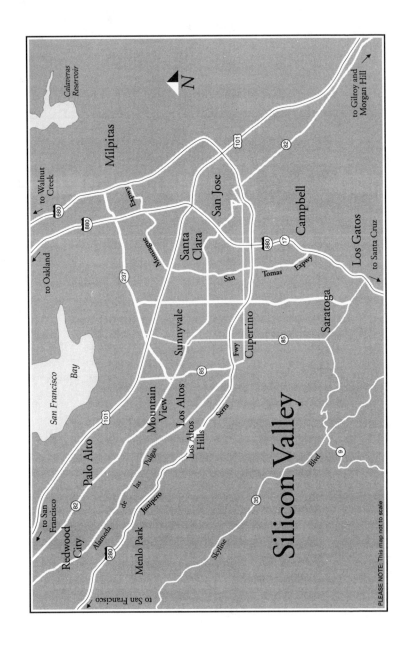

Silicon Valley

PLEASE NOTE: This map not to scale

Table of Contents

Introduction

Welcome to Silicon Valley.

What is it? America's — perhaps the world's — greatest accumulation of technological talent and research/development facilities, the birthplace of the information- and data-driven Technology Revolution that is changing life in the 20th Century just as profoundly as the Industrial Revolution changed life in the 18th and 19th Centuries.

Where is it? There still is debate about the epicenter of this new revolution. It may be Stanford University, where Professor Frederick Terman's instructional inspiration helped begin the germination process. It may be Palo Alto, where William Hewlett and David Packard got their start in a simple garage workshop. It may be Mountain View, where Robert Noyce, at William Shockley's Shockley Labs, invented the integrated circuit.

But there is no debate over the source of the name Silicon Valley — it was coined in the 1960s by newsletter publisher Don Hoefler — and there is no debate over Hoefler's reasoning — that so much silicon suddenly was being used to fabricate wafers for those semiconductors and integrated circuits that what formerly had been known only as the Santa Clara Valley might now be called Silicon Valley, both alliteratively and realistically. Since the Santa Clara Valley of California encompasses Stanford University and Palo Alto and Mountain View—and the state's third largest city, San Jose, as well—for all practical purposes (and the purpose of this book), Santa Clara Valley and Silicon Valley are synonymous.

Why visit Silicon Valley? The reasons are many: the excitement of being where the cutting edge of the future is honed; the natural beauty of a valley cradling the southern portion of San Francisco Bay between the redwood-lush Santa Cruz Mountains on the west and the oak-studded Diablo Range on the east; the accommodating climate, where temperatures are seldom extreme and humidity seldom is a concern.

But most compelling is the lure of history, the sense of participation in epochal events. It's presumptuous, of course, to predict what future historians will say, but given the effect of the innovations developed in Silicon Valley on the rest of the world thus far, it's not far-fetched to think that some day the region might well be compared to Florence, Italy at the start of the Renaissance. Being here—being able to say you where here when . . . —is an opportunity not to be missed.

1
A Basic High-Tech Primer

To understand Silicon Valley, it's first necessary to understand the technology involved. What developments brought so many bright people together in one place in such a short time to record such a wide range of accomplishments? The language used to describe what they do can sound arcane — gate arrays, complementary metal oxide silicon, CAD/CAM, geometric lithography. Even basic English is changed so that "access" becomes a verb and "input" a noun. But don't let that throw you. All or most of high technology either starts with, or is related to, a simple item with which almost everyone is familiar: a switch.

You throw a switch to turn the lights off or on. Technicians work to do the same thing, only faster and smaller and cheaper. The evolution of this switch has been from mechanical to electro-mechanical to electric to electronic and, experimentally, to atomic, but the basic task remains the same: off and on.

In the beginning was the simple switch, the kind you throw by hand. That's mechanical.

Next came the discovery that you need not be physically present to throw that switch; electrical current could be used to create a mechanical field that would throw the switch for you. That's electro-mechanical.

Next, it was discovered that you really didn't need that

3

switch to perform the off/on function — just keep the magnet and reverse its magnetic field when you wanted the job done. The best way to do that was by using two plates, firing charged electrons between them, back and forth, in a vacuum. That's electric.

Then, scientists found that even a vacuum wasn't necessary. Instead, they could wrap plates with a material between them that had been chemically treated or "doped" to give it limited conductivity (hence "semiconductor"). By using electricity to vary the conductivity of this solid-state material, you can make a switch that way — the transistor.

Eventually, other scientists realized they could take these transistors, lay them out flat and duplicate them over and over, using photographic processes, into a combination of switches. That's electronic — the integrated circuit.

These individual circuits, each with a different task, were wired together on a plastic board into groups, called systems, and each system has bred others. There are instruments made of these devices, instruments to test these devices, instruments that contain these devices and instruments that . . . well, anyone who has ever been in a hall of mirrors knows how it works.

Each of these breakthroughs has roughly followed Moore's Law: that every year, the ratio of power to size to price improves by 30 percent. Thus, last year's computer is replaced by one that is 30 percent more powerful for the same price, or one that is 30 percent smaller for the same price. That has been going on for more than 30 years.

The result: If the time it takes you to manually throw that switch is one second and an electro-mechanical switch can do the job in one-tenth of a second, then that electrical tube can do it in one-hundredth of a second, an early transistor in one-thousandth of a second and modern integrated circuits in one nanosecond (one-billionth of a second).

Likewise, a computer small enough to sit on your lap that currently sells for less than $600 is more powerful than an IBM mainframe computer of 1953, which filled up most of a large room and cost $4 million.

Modern mainframes have a memory of more than 1 trillion bytes and operate in the 5-nanosecond or faster range. These mainframes are being linked into combinations that can do even more even faster. And scientists have shown it's possible to reduce the size of that switch to a pair of single atoms.

But it's still just a switch.

And that switch obviously still is on.

2
Tech Talk

What's with all that jargon, that stuff about bytes and such? Engineers started it, sales and support people picked it up, and today you can hardly carry on a conversation in Silicon Valley without coming across terms that in other settings would be esoteric and arcane. Here are some elementary definitions of common technical terms to help you sound like a native — or cope with one:

Bit: a condensed term for "binary digit," either a 1 or a 0, the smallest unit of information recognized by computers and the form in which they store data.

Byte: a group of bits, usually eight in number, that together form a single character of computer memory. Computers' memory size is measured in kilobytes (1,024 bytes) or megabytes (about 1 million bytes).

CAD/CAM: (pronounced "cad cam"), acronyms for Computer Assisted Design and Computer Assisted Manufacturing.

CD-ROM: (pronounced "see dee rom"), a high-density compact disk-like disk used for memory storage, especially in multi-media applications.

Chip: integrated circuits, microscopic electrical pathways chemically etched and implanted with metals on tiny slivers of silicon.

7

CMOS: (pronounced "see moss"), acronym for Complementary Metal Oxide Semiconductor, integrated circuits with complementary transistors on the same wafer, allowing for low power dissipation.

Disk: a computer memory device. Either rigid, known as hard disks, or flexible, known as floppies, they store information on magnetized iron-oxide coatings.

DRAM: (pronounced "dee ram"), acronym for Dynamic Random Access Memory, the main memory chips in almost all computers.

Fab: short for fabrication, the physical process of manufacturing chips.

Gate Array: a type of customer-designed integrated circuit. A similar technology is ASIC (Application-Specific Integrated Circuit.)

Mainframe: the largest, speediest and most expensive class of computers.

Massively Parallel Computer: a computing technique in which large numbers of small processors work in parallel to solve problems rapidly.

Memory chip: an integrated circuit that stores data. There are two commonly used types: random-access memory (or RAM), chips that store information temporarily and allow it to be manipulated by the user; and read-only memory (or ROM), chips that store information permanently and cannot be altered by the user.

Megabyte: (or meg, or mb), is the equivalent of 1 million bytes.

Microprocessor: combinations of integrated circuits that form the brains of electronic devices such as computers, allowing such devices to process data through calculations and logical decisions; literally, a tiny processor or computer on a chip.

Multi-media: more recent personal computer technology

that combines sound and, in the best case, full motion video.

Multiprocessing: a computer design in which two or more processing units are coupled together to run different programs simultaneously while sharing the same computer frame and memory.

Personal Computer: (or PC), smaller, less expensive desktop computers for home use, as opposed to the mainframe computers used for commercial purposes.

RISC: (pronounced "risk"), acronym for Reduced Instruction Set Computer, in which microprocessors use smaller sets of instructions, usually limited to those instructions used most often, for greater efficiency.

Semiconductor: commonly a material such as silicon whose ability to conduct electricity can be either increased or lessened by chemical treatment, making it possible to contain complex circuits in microscopic size.

Supercomputer: a large computer with very high performance capability and, usually, a multi-million dollar cost.

Transistor: semiconducting material sandwiched between two points that act like an on-off switch to process data.

Wafer: a circular sheet of silicon upon which numerous chips can be etched at the same time, then cut apart into individual integrated circuits.

Workstation: a high-end desktop computer largely used for CAD/CAM-type applications. In many areas, it has supplanted the minicomputer.

3
Modern History

Historical memory can be short in California, whose huge influx of new residents almost makes it appear that most people moved here last week. But that's appropriate for Silicon Valley, where a company, as in the case of Gavilan Computer, can grow from nothing to a $100 million business and then disappear into nothingness again, all in 18 months.

Seeds of the valley's technological development were planted in the 1930s and 1940s, primarily in the Stanford University engineering department headed by Frederick Terman. His evangelical insistence on combining the theoretical with the practical fell on the receptive ears of such students as William Hewlett, David Packard, and Sigurd and Russell Varian. They put it into practice when the demands of World War II for such products as Varian Associates' klystron tube (a key component of a then-new device known as radar), and Hewlett-Packard's electronics measuring equipment helped boost those fledgling companies onto a growth curve that others wanted to emulate.

It was also in the 1940s that the transistor was invented by William Shockley, William Brattwin and John Burdeen at Bell Labs in New Jersey. But it was other firms, among them Shockley Labs in Palo Alto (Shockley had moved back home), that turned that invention into a commercially viable commodity, and provided a breeding ground for further innovative talent. Likewise, the region's war-time connections with defense and aeronautics continued into the post-war period of heavy population growth, when companies such as Lockheed's missiles and space division settled in Sunnyvale and grew into Santa Clara County's largest employer today.

By the 1950s, a critical mass of brainpower and investment capital was being reached. In 1957, eight engineers left Shockley Labs to found a new company, Fairchild Semiconductor, and one of the eight, Robert Noyce, developed the concept of the integrated circuit, or microchip. Fairchild, in turn, spun off more start-up electronics firms that would grow into giants, with W.J. "Jerry" Sanders helping found Advanced Micro Devices, and with Charles Sporck launching National Semiconductor. Eventually Noyce also departed and joined with Andrew Grove and Gordon Moore at Intel to pursue new chip technologies that would, in time, lead to the microprocessor.

As part of the process, already-established electronics firms such as IBM launched operations here, wanting to be where the action was. New companies and new industries continued to be born. For example, Nolan Bushnell's Pong catapulted the electronic game craze and made, for a time, his Atari company a household word.

A valley that once had been largely agricultural was transforming itself into a technological beehive. Among the most spectacular examples of this was the 1977 birth of the personal computer industry, appropriately launched in a Cupertino garage by Steve Jobs and Steve Wozniak. Both only in their 20s, they had met in an informal computer club and pooled their knowledge and enthusiasm to create a computer for the individual, not just the corporation or laboratory.

And the creative process accelerated. By 1980 there were 179,000 persons working in electronics in Silicon Valley; by

1990, there were 221,700. The average after-tax income per household in 1989 topped $50,000, a 64 percent increase in fewer than ten years. Between 1981 and 1990, venture capitalists had invested more than $4 billion to get new electronics companies started in the area, and during that same period 128 of those firms had grown enough to make initial public stock offerings. At the start of this decade, more than 700 Silicon Valley electronics companies had annual sales of $5 million or more.

More numbers? Sure. Santa Clara County ranks third in the nation in median household effective buying income ($45,662), and the San Jose Metropolitan Area ranks third nationally in percentage (44.9 percent) of households with incomes of $50,000 or more. The county's industries lead the United States in production of electron tubes (25 percent of the nation's total output), semiconductors and related devices (23 percent) and computer storage devices (22 percent). The metropolitan area is home to more than 3,000 high technology companies employing nearly 230,000 persons. In fact, one of every three workers in the county is employed in manufacturing. It's a hard-working area.

"The whole world looks to Silicon Valley as the departure point for the future of technology," Philippe Kahn, the president of Borland International, has been quoted in Forbes magazine. "If you go to France, they tell you they're trying to make a French Silicon Valley, and the same in Germany, and the same in Japan. But nobody else has been able to do it."

The secret to that Silicon Valley success lies in part with its universities: Stanford, San Jose State and Santa Clara. Stanford, as noted previously, provided the initial intellectual spark and continues to provide both inspiration and innovation. San Jose State, the largest of the three, has provided the bulk of the technological workforce and through its Applied Technology Institute for Microelectronics creates an umbrella for formal industry-education-government partnerships aimed at technological development. And Santa Clara, by stressing instruction not only in engineering but also in business, law and ethics, offers valuable balance and leavening to the heady mix of creation and computing. Add in nearby campuses of San Francisco State and the Universities of California at Berkeley and Santa Cruz, and you have an educational mix capable of providing fine intellectual ferment.

Another major part of the Silicon Valley equation is its people, the best and brightest in a variety of disciplines, attracted by that intellectual ferment and the knowledge that working here is synonymous with fast-track career development. Another Forbes magazine quote, this time from T.J. Rodgers of Cypress Semiconductor: "You can find good R&D (research and development) people in plenty of places. What makes Silicon Valley different is that R&D and manufacturing and marketing and money can all sit down at the same table and ask, 'What if . . . ?' "

Add to that the benign nature of the valley itself — a temperate climate that lets residents concentrate on more important things than surviving boiling heat or bone-chilling cold — and the increasingly diverse population, and Silicon Valley becomes not only a unique American treasure but also an international centerpiece. "Foreign investors know their people can come here and find doctors, lawyers, department stores and grocery stores that understand their language and their needs," says David Gould of Fujitsu. "That's a very large plus."

What's next from the valley that has brought the world the transistor, the semiconductor, the microprocessor, the personal computer and the videocassette recorder? The answer may lie in the minds of that small group of engineers huddled over a back table in a Mountain View diner, or on the workbench of yet another garage in San Jose, or in a start-up company in neighboring San Mateo, Santa Cruz and southern Alameda counties, where high-tech firms are expanding amoeba-like beyond the original valley. But if the track record of the recent past is any indicator, it'll make history.

The 100-Mile Historical Silicon Circuit

Want a first-hand look at Silicon Valley's roots? They're spread throughout the area — this is California, after all, and sprawl is a way of life. So get your car ready — once again, this is California where few walk if they can drive. Pack a lunch, perhaps, for you'll pass perfect places both rural and urban for a picnic, or plan on dining at one of the many restaurants en route, for this trip can take all day. Use the map located at the end of this chapter to trace the following circular drive of technological history. Call it the Silicon Valley Circuit.

Begin in downtown San Jose — appropriately at the circle of palm trees on South Market Street between the Fairmont Hotel and the San Jose Museum of Art where San Jose became the first capital of California. Look across the plaza for the brass plaque on the side of the Silicon Valley Plaza tower, marking:

1. **Herrold broadcasting station,** First and San Fernando Streets, San Jose. A reminder that there were technological innovations here even before the 1930s. In 1909 from an office in the former Garden City Bank building at this intersection, Charles Herrold made radio history by becoming the first person to transmit radio programs of music and news to a listening audience.

Then drive south on Market Street past more strip commercial establishments than you'll ever want to see again, noticing that the name of the street eventually changes to Monterey Highway, until you approach Blossom Hill and Cottle roads and you see on your right:

2. **IBM,** 5600 Cottle Rd., San Jose. The main plant of Big Blue's Silicon Valley complex and a player, although more old-line and conservatively corporate than the rest, in the growth of Silicon Valley since the '50s. It was here, in IBM's Winchester division that the first computer disk memories were designed—hence the Santa Clara Valley-named "Winchester" drives that fill modern personal computers.

Follow the highway signs for the U.S. 101 Freeway north, following it until the Yerba Buena exit. Continue right on Yerba Buena Road until you see nestled in the rolling California terrain:

3. **Montgomery Hill,** 3095 Yerba Buena Rd., San Jose. Here a plaque at the entrance to Evergreen Valley College marks the spot where aviation pioneer John J. Montgomery died in an airplane crash in 1911. One of the valley's first scientifically oriented innovators, Montgomery was the first to demonstrate that man could indeed soar like the birds by flying gliders.

Return to San Felipe Road, turn right and follow it to Aborn Road where you'll turn left. Another left turn on Capitol Expressway will return you to U.S. 101 North (follow the San Francisco signs). Continue north on the 101 freeway through San Jose and Santa Clara, and take the Lawrence Expressway South exit into Sunnyvale. Follow Lawrence Expressway south to:

4. **Arques Avenue,** where a right turn will take you past the acres of tilt-up concrete-construction buildings on what once were prune and apricot orchards. These are R&D

(research and development) parks, exhibiting architecture typical of Silicon Valley's explosive growth in the 1960s, and demonstrating the construction techniques still used today.

Turn right on Fair Oaks Avenue, following it across the 101 Freeway as its name changes to Java Avenue, and then turn left on Borregas Ave. to:

5. **Atari,** 1196 Borregas, Sunnyvale. Its meteoric growth as a video game developer/manufacturer—and its equally precipitous decline and sale—still rank as Silicon Valley's greatest rags-to-riches-to-rags story. Not everyone gets rich—or stays rich—here.

Continue on Borregas to Moffett Park Drive, then turn right and near its intersection with Mathilda Avenue you will see almost straight ahead:

6. **Lockheed,** 1111 Lockheed Way, Sunnyvale. Lockheed's Missiles and Space Division is Silicon Valley's largest employer, largely through putting technology to work in defense applications. Particularly note the square, blue building—the "Blue Cube," officially Onizuka Air Force Base—where for decades the Air Force has directed satellite eyes-in-the-sky to peek earthward on friends and enemies.

Turn left on Mathilda, re-cross U.S. 101 and continue to Maude Avenue, where you'll turn left again. A right turn onto Sunnyvale Avenue and a left turn on Hendy Avenue will bring you to:

7. **Hendy Iron Works/Westinghouse,** 501 Hendy Ave., Sunnyvale. One of Santa Clara Valley's early industrial plants (it moved here after the San Francisco earthquake and fire of 1906), Hendy transmogrified into Westinghouse, typical of the shift toward technology and the Silicon Valley label

that accompanied it. There's a small museum here with exhibits charting that growth.

Then backtrack on Hendy (it's a dead-end street) to Sunnyvale Avenue again, turn left and follow it to El Camino Real. Turn right and almost immediately on your right you will see:

8. Rooster T. Feathers, now a comedy club at 157 W. El Camino Real, Sunnyvale. But when it was a watering hole known as Andy Capp's, that's where Nolan Bushnell introduced the first video game, Pong. He initially thought the experiment was a failure when the club's manager called to say the game wasn't working. Then Bushnell discovered why — the machine was so jammed with quarters that no more could be accepted — and he knew he had a hit on his hands.

Continue northward on El Camino Real to State Route 85 North (again, follow the signs for San Francisco) and follow 85 northward until you see on your right as it merges with U.S. 101:

9. NASA/Ames Research Facility, Moffett Blvd. at Highway 101, Mountain View. The business of space exploration is brought down to earth here through research carried on with such esoteric equipment as a mammoth wind tunnel (located inside that huge building with the diamond-shaped construction grids on its exterior) and a flight simulator laboratory. Tours are available, but require advance reservation. And if you're wondering about those mammoth curved-top structures adjacent on the land of Moffett Naval Air Station, they're dirigible hangars, built to house the lighter-than-air leviathans of the 1920s and 1930s.

Follow U.S. 101 North (those San Francisco-direction signs again) to the Rengstorff Avenue exit, where you'll turn right almost immediately to loop onto Charleston Rd. Turn left on Charleston and follow it across San Antonio Road to:

10. **Site of Fairchild,** 844 East Charleston Rd., Palo Alto. A historical marker here commemorates this unprepossessing industrial building as the start of Silicon Valley's first industrial park and the company that, led by Shockley Labs refugee Robert Noyce, spawned the semiconductor industry, as well as more than 150 spin-off companies.

Backtrack on Charleston to San Antonio Road, and turn right, following it to, on your left:

11. **Site of Shockley Labs,** 391 San Antonio Rd., Mountain View, now occupied by a Sound Goods store. This site was the birthplace of the modern Silicon Valley and the training ground for a generation of corporate titans-to-be.

Continue on San Antonio Road to El Camino Real and turn right, following northward into Palo Alto, where you'll turn left on Page Mill Road and pass through:

12. **Stanford Industrial Park,** symbolic of Silicon Valley's innovative interaction between the worlds of academe and commerce, a veritable "who's who" of technology plants and the place where Russell and Sigurd Varian first set up shop. When French President Charles de Gaulle visited the West Coast, he specifically asked to see the Stanford Industrial Park. Why shouldn't you?

Continue on Page Mill Road to Junipero Serra Boulevard, where you'll turn right. Pass Campus Drive East and turn right on Campus Drive West, the site of:

13. **Movies' birthplace.** It was near here, on a race track adjacent to a horse barn on Leland Stanford's farm in 1878 and 1879 that photographer Eadweard Muybridge set up a

lineup of 24 cameras, rigged to trip-wires that snapped a series of photographs as a race horse ran past. The photos proved that horses, in full stride, at times have all four hooves off the ground. And in the process, the photos, when arranged on a circular wheel, could be spun to give the appearance of motion—not precisely what motion pictures are today, but a tantalizing and historic glimpse of what was to come.

Follow Campus Drive West as it winds through:

14. Stanford University. The school of higher learning founded in 1881 by railroad tycoon Leland Stanford in memory of his son, is among other things, the site of Prof. Frederick Terman's lab (you'll see signs directing you to it on your right) where such Silicon Valley pillars as Russell and Sigurd Varian, David Packard and Bill Hewlett later got their push toward success.

Turn left off Campus Drive West onto Palm Avenue, exiting the campus and crossing El Camino Real, and then follow the signs for Alma Street and loop to your right. Turn left onto Alma and follow it to Addison Street, where you turn left again and soon come to:

15. The Hewlett-Packard Garage, at 367 Addison St., Palo Alto. Here the partnership between Bill Hewlett and David Packard began its earliest tinkering, developing in 1938 an oscillator used by Walt Disney to improve the sound quality on his animated motion picture, *Fantasia*. The 12-by-18 foot building is now a state historical landmark.

Continue on Addison to Middlefield Road, turn left and follow it through the high-rent Palo Alto and Menlo Park suburbs into Redwood City, where you'll turn right onto Marsh Road (there's a right-turn lane, not terribly well marked by a white wooden post sign; if you find yourself in Redwood City's Hispanic business district, you've gone too far). Follow Marsh Road to Fair Oaks Avenue, turn left and continue to Second Avenue, where you'll turn right. Follow Second Avenue to Broadway, turn left, and almost immediately on your left you will see:

16. **Ampex Corp.,** 401 Broadway, Redwood City. Innovative engineer Alexander Poniatoff originally started in San Carlos, selling electrical generators and motors to the Navy in World War II, but when he put his mind to work on post-war consumer products — the first American audio tape recorder, plus the technology behind videotape, electronic tape-editing and instant-replay — his company grew into the sprawling 55-acre campus, complete with public museum, that you see today. Unfortunately for Ampex and the American economy, the company licensed all of these technologies to the Japanese.

Continue northward on Broadway to State Route 84, Woodside Road, and turn left. Follow Woodside Road westward to the Interstate 280 Freeway and go south (toward San Jose). Exit I-280 at the Sand Hill Road East off-ramp and, heading eastward, look left to:

17. **3000 Sand Hill Road,** Menlo Park. Long the center of venture capital activity for Silicon Valley, the Sun Deck cafeteria here is the place to talk cash and coffee. In Hollywood, the people all would be carrying scripts. Here, they're carrying business plans and spreadsheets.

Then, as you continue east on Sand Hill Road, look right to see:

18. **Stanford Linear Accelerator Center,** 2575 Sand Hill Rd., Palo Alto. A racetrack for atoms, two miles long and extending back under that more ordinary racetrack — the Interstate

280. Here scientists probe the inner workings of the universe's building blocks. It's also the former meeting place of the Homebrew Computer Club, a loosely organized group of budding computer whizzes that once counted young Steve Wozniak and Steve Jobs, the founders of Apple, among its members.

Then turn right off Sand Hill Road onto Alpine Road (confusingly, if you were to turn left at this intersection you'd be on Santa Cruz Avenue). Continue on Alpine, following the signs for Portola Valley, until you come to Interstate 280 again. Take I-280 South (toward San Jose once more). Exit at Saratoga-Sunnyvale Road, heading right into Cupertino and the midst of:

19. **Apple's core.** The street name changes to De Anza Boulevard between I-280 and Stevens Creek Boulevard, Cupertino, home of Apple Computer. Apple, which launched the personal computer industry, has lots of buildings in lots of places, but the structures along this stretch of roadway comprise the heart of its empire.

Continue on De Anza Boulevard as its name changes to Saratoga-Sunnyvale Road (State Route 9) again and follow it past Saratoga into Los Gatos, where it chauvinistically becomes Los Gatos-Saratoga Road. Turn left on University Avenue, following it across Blossom Hill Road until, as you see the waters of Lake Vasona on your right you come to the site of:

20. **Eagle's tragedy.** Fledgling Eagle Computer went public in 1983, making president Dennis Barnhart an instant millionaire. There were a few celebratory drinks, he went out for a spin in his new Ferrari along this stretch of University Avenue winding past Vasona Reservoir. The car flipped over an embankment. Barnhart died in the crash.

Thus sobered, follow University Avenue to Lark Avenue. Turn right, following Lark eastward to State Highway 17 North (the San Jose direction again). Take the Highway 17 freeway north to I-280 South (the Downtown San Jose signs), then south on I-280 to Guadalupe Expressway. Exit on Guadalupe to the Santa Clark Street off-ramp. Go right on Santa Clark Street to Market Street and right again on Market to San Antonio Street, where your odyssey began.

By now, you've had a good look at Silicon Valley — historically, geographically and automotively. Get out and stretch your legs. You've earned it.

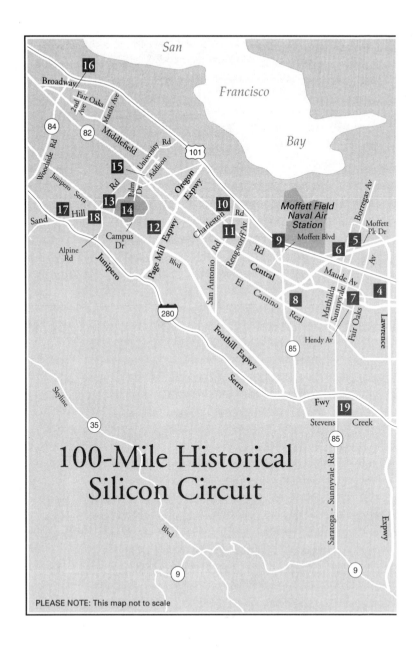

100-Mile Historical Silicon Circuit

PLEASE NOTE: This map not to scale

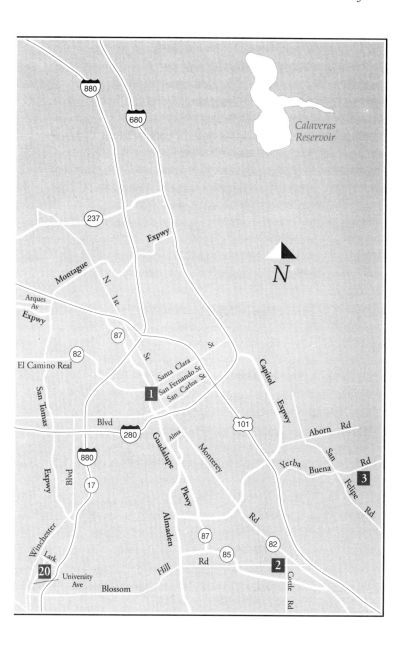

4
Ancient History

This is California, right? The state of new arrivals, where ancient history is anything that happened before you got here and three-year residents qualify as "old-timers."

Still, knowing something more about what went on before Santa Clara Valley became Silicon Valley — or before it became Santa Clara Valley — helps fill out one's perspective. So let's take it from the top:

The first people to inhabit the part of California we now call Silicon Valley trudged across the then land bridge from Asia to North America, anthropologists say. Some eventually walked all the way into Central and South America, but enough stopped off in California, with its pleasant climate and ample food supply, to set up a fairly extensive culture. The Ohlone, as they were called in California, flourished here from perhaps 7,000 B.C. until 1800 A.D., at one time reaching a peak population (in 1777) of 9,000 persons living around San Francisco Bay.

Then the Europeans made their entrance, exploring the "new world." Sir Francis Drake sailed the California coast on behalf of his British queen. Russian explorers followed the original people's trail down from the north as far as Fort Ross. But it was the Spanish who exerted the most influence. Operating from a stronghold in Mexico, Spain began colonizing northward with Father Junipero Serra seeking converts for the Catholic Church, and the Spanish Army seeking territory, leading the way.

The principal explorer of Silicon Valley was Captain Gaspar de Portola, sent north from San Diego by Serra to check out reports that Monterey Bay might be a good spot for a new mission. Portola was either inadequate for the task or possessed an inaccurate map. He missed Monterey Bay entirely and continued north until he stopped near what now is Half Moon Bay before realizing he'd missed the turnoff. Two soldiers were dispatched into the foothills to search for food and a way out of their mess, when from the summit of Sweeney Ridge in Pacifica they looked eastward to discover a wondrous sight—the lush Santa Clara Valley stretching out before them to their right and, to their left and center, what had to be a bay classier than Monterey's—San Francisco Bay. Portola realized he had lucked-out so he scouted the region, made copious notes and then high-tailed it back to San Diego to report his findings, missing Monterey Bay again on the way to keep his record intact.

Was Father Serra pleased? Not exactly. "You have been to Rome," he reportedly said with a sigh to Portola, "without seeing the Pope." So much for Gaspar, although he did leave his mark; Portola Valley, in the hills between Stanford University and the Pacific Ocean, today is one of Silicon Valley's prime residential areas with homesites as valued as the gold the Spanish sought.

Serra, of course, ended up in all the history books and is buried in Mission Carmel Borromeo on Monterey Bay (other explorers eventually found the place). He also is memorialized by a monumental statue by sculptor Louis Dubois, erected in 1976 alongside Interstate 280 near, of all places, Portola Valley. The statue shows Serra on one knee, pointing vaguely seaward. (In November as the "Big Game" football meeting between Stanford and rival University of

California, Berkeley, approaches, students have been known to stick a giant papier-mache football beneath that outstretched finger, making it appear that Serra is holding the ball for the point-after-touchdown.)

In 1776, while colonists and settlers on the other side of the continent were kicking up a fuss, the Spanish sent an explorer other than Portola—one Juan Bautista de Anza—back northward to the San Francisco Bay area to select mission sites. De Anza didn't get lost, chose a couple of promising spots for what would become the missions Santa Clara de Asis and Dolores, and got his name into the history books as the founder of San Francisco, which formed around the latter mission.

On January 12, 1777, Mission Santa Clara de Asis came into physical being. The original buildings didn't last, falling victim to a series of fires. Today only a wooden cross facing a reconstruction of the mission church remains located on the grounds of Santa Clara University. The mission did serve to give its name to the valley, however. It also became the catalyst for development of the region; the Spanish civil authorities decided to establish a settlement nearby to raise cattle and other foodstuffs for the soldiers at the presidios (forts) guarding San Francisco and Monterey Bays. The outpost, the Pueblo de San Jose, thus became California's first civil settlement, founded November 29, 1777.

The next 50 years or so were a mixed bag, a good news/bad news situation for the Spanish.

The bad news: The mission priests tried to bend the Ohlone people to a more regimented, European way of life, in the process uprooting them from their villages and moving them onto the mission grounds and out of the way of the developing city of San Jose. Few of the Ohlone—or their fellow tribespeople—were suited to the type of life the missionaries envisioned for them here on earth. Their low resistance to the disease organisms carried by the Europeans, however, sent great numbers of Ohlone to the life the priests had promised them in the hereafter. (By 1900, the native American population of the Bay Area had shrunk to fewer than 1,000).

The good news: While the missionaries were saving souls but losing converts, the farmers had found the rich bottom soil of the valley to be perfectly suited for crops, and their fortunes prospered. This disparity wasn't lost on the Spanish (now Mexican) rulers of Alta California. In 1833, Mexico passed a law ostensibly transferring all mission lands, except churches, out of the control of the Catholic Church and into the hands of the Ohlone. Noble in principle, but in practice the land quickly was divided into ranchos and taken over by whomever knew best how to get through the courts of law. (Clue: It wasn't the Ohlone; only three grants were made to native Americans in the valley.)

The land deals satisfied the local power structure, if not the Pope or the Ohlone, but there were problems for Mexico. By 1836, when Mission Santa Clara was secularized, hordes of settlers from the United States were moving westward. In 1844, there arrived in the Santa Clara Valley Martin Murphy Sr. and Elisha Stephens, leading a train of 100 wagons over the Sierra Nevada. Martin Murphy Sr. bought a rancho in Morgan Hill; his son Martin Jr., bought what now is the city of Sunnyvale (the Mexican rancheros weren't above making a real estate deal or two). Stephens picked up the part of Cupertino now known as the Blackberry Farm, but didn't have enough good fortune to get a road named properly for him (Stevens Creek Boulevard is a historical misspelling).

Still other non-Mexicans flocked here in 1844 when a Mexican mining engineer discovered quicksilver (mercury) in the hills at the south end of the valley. The Ohlone had used the reddish cinnabar for makeup, but canny miners recognized that the mineral had even greater value as a major agent in the reduction process for extracting gold and silver. They named the region New Almaden, after Almaden in south-central Spain, site of the world's largest quicksilver mine. The choice of names wasn't grandiose as the New Almaden mine eventually yielded more than $70,000 in ore to the Cornish, Welsh, English, American and Spanish miners who worked its veins. It also broke the virtual world monopoly on quicksilver, held by the British banking house of Rothschild.

By 1848 there were enough American settlers and disaffected Mexican residents in California to make possible the Bear Flag Revolution and the secession of the region from Mexico, setting the stage for its inclusion into the Union as the 31st state. In 1849, gold was discovered and California's population zoomed.

San Jose was briefly the new state's first capital, but being too far from the center of activity in the gold country of the Sierra foothills, it eventually lost out to Sacramento as the seat of state government.

So, the Santa Clara Valley opted to switch from gold to purple; when Louis Pellier introduced the French prune to the region in 1856, it flourished beyond his wildest dreams. Before long the valley was a veritable sea of orchards, producing some of the finest prunes and, later, apricots in the world. In 1870, Dr. James Dawson canned the first fruit on a stove in a shed near his San Jose home at The Alameda and Polhemus Street. This was the beginning of the fruit canning industry, and San Jose soon became the state's fruit-shipping capital.

It was a lovely, quiet and bucolic existence, which lasted until the entry of the United States into World War II. That sent floods of servicemen and women pouring through West Coast ports, destined for battle in the Pacific Theater. Many saw the lovely, quiet, idyllic valley with its miles of flowering fruit trees and vowed to return there—if they returned at all. After the war, return many did. So many that life in the valley changed forever.

Example: At the start of the war, the population of the Santa Clara Valley's county seat, San Jose, was 68,457, and the population of the county itself was 174,949. By 1960, only fifteen years after the war's end, San Jose had ballooned to a city of 202,571 and the county had a population of 642,315.

The people who had come to live in a little cottage with an orchard view were living in what once had been the orchards themselves. The county's cities went on a binge of more than five-hundred land annexations. No longer was it possible to tell where San Jose stopped and the suburbs began; everything was flowing together into a megalopolis.

Urban planners still look aghast at this period of explosive growth. Then again, urban planners usually look aghast at anything they themselves didn't plan, and the westward tilt that poured people into California certainly was more of a natural force than the sterile theories of zoning and land-use.

True, the valley no longer looked like a sea of blossoms in the spring, but in the sea of people that replaced them were the seeds of a different type of growth altogether: the brainpower that reached critical mass and blossomed into the inventive marvel of Silicon Valley.

A lot has happened since that first Ohlone told his wife (or vice versa), "Forget the hike to Mexico this summer, dear. This looks like a better place to stop."

It still is.

Historical Highlights

Clyde Arbuckle, city historian of San Jose, suggests the following ten places to visit for a well-rounded picture of the Santa Clara Valley's roots:

Alviso. Now a district of San Jose but from 1849 to 1864, it served as the main port of entry to the valley. Today it is cluttered with boatworks, restaurants, residences and marinas in need of frequent dredging. To reach it, drive north from San Jose on First Street until it ends at the southern edge of San Francisco Bay.

Henry W. Coe State Park. For a peek at how the California landscape looked before the arrival of Europeans — rolling oat grass-covered hills, oak trees and manzanita brush, with hiking trails for those who wish to get really close. Fourteen miles east of Morgan Hill on East Dunne Avenue. Tel: 408/779-2728.

Hakone Gardens. A classic Japanese-style garden-cum-park, a serene example of the valley's Asian heritage. Big Basin Road, one-quarter mile south of Saratoga Village. Tel: 408/741-1689.

Lick Observatory. Established in 1888 atop 4,209' Mount Hamilton in the Diablo Range rimming Santa Clara Valley to the east, it is the nation's first permanently occupied mountain observatory. Philanthropist James Lick is buried there. Reached from San Jose by taking Alum Rock Avenue east to Mount Hamilton Road and thence upward to the observatory at 7281 Mount Hamilton Road. Not a trip for those prone to car-sickness. Tel: 408/274-5061.

New Almaden. Quicksilver mines of worldwide significance. Almaden Quicksilver Park, a good focal point for the village located in south San Jose, is located at 21785 Almaden Road. Tel: 408/268-8220.

San Jose State University. Founded in 1857, this is the oldest public institution of higher education on the Pacific Coast. Located at 1 Washington Square, a 97-acre grid in downtown San Jose, with the intersection of San Fernando and South Fourth Streets a good place to begin exploration. Tel: 408/924-6350.

Santa Clara University. Founded in 1851 by the Society of Jesus, this is the first Pacific Coast institution to offer classes in higher education. Site of a replica of the original Mission Santa Clara de Asis, the eighth of California's 21 missions. 500 El Camino Real, Santa Clara. Tel: 408/554-4000.

Skyline Boulevard. A hilltop-clinging road, often narrow and winding, through the Santa Cruz Mountains. It offers vistas to the east of the Santa Clara Valley, much as the first Spanish explorers may have seen them. You may want to follow it from its intersection with La Honda Road in Portola Valley on the north to its southern terminus at Bear Creek Road for the best views.

Stanford University. Opened in 1891 by railroad magnate Leland Stanford and wife Jane as a memorial to their only son, Leland Jr., who died of typhoid in 1884. El Camino Real at University Avenue, Palo Alto. Tel: 415/723-5631.

Winchester Mystery House. The former home of firearms heiress Sarah Winchester. See it for its architecture; the "mystery" part may be more fancy than fact. 525 Winchester Blvd., San Jose. Tel: 408/247-2101.

Best of the Rest

HISTORICAL MUSEUMS. Some worth visiting for additional perspective are:

California History Center. Archives and exhibits with an emphasis on Santa Clara Valley History. De Anza College, 21250 Stevens Creek Blvd., Cupertino. Tel: 408/864-8712. Open Mon.-Fri., 8 a.m. to 4:30 p.m. Closed July and August.

Campbell Historical Museum. Artifacts of city and regional past. 51 North Central Ave. and Civic Center Dr., Campbell. Tel: 408/866-2119. Open Tues.-Sat., 1:30 to 4:30 p.m.

Los Gatos Museum. Artifacts of city and regional past; art exhibitions. Main and Tait Streets, Los Gatos. Tel: 408/354-

2646. Open Tues.-Sun., 10 a.m. to 4 p.m.

Museum of American Heritage. Patriotic exhibits; electrical and mechanical collections of past 100 years. 275 Alma St., Palo Alto. Tel: 415/321-1004. Open Fri.-Sun, 11 a.m. to 4 p.m.

San Jose Historical Museum. Reconstruction of portion of turn-of-the- century San Jose, archives, and exhibits. Kelley Park, Senter Rd. and Phelan Ave., San Jose. Tel: 408/287-2290. Open Mon.-Fri., 10 a.m-4:30 p.m.; Sat. and Sun., 12-4:30 p.m.

Sunnyvale Historical Museum. Artifacts of city history, displayed on the site of the original Murphy residence. 235 East California Ave., Sunnyvale. Tel: 408/749-0220. Open Tues.-Thurs., 12-3:30 and Sun., 1-4 p.m.

WALKING TOUR

Additionally, San Jose offers a self-guided historical walking tour of the city center, with maps available from the visitor information office inside the San Jose McEnery Convention Center, 150 West San Carlos St., 408/295-9600. The tour starts at Plaza Park, facing the San Jose Fairmont Hotel, with descriptive markers indicating the following points of interest:

Plaza Park, a portion of the original plaza of the 1797 Pueblo de San Jose and the oldest continuously used public open space in the city.

Chinatown, across South Market Street from the Plaza, now largely the site of the Fairmont Hotel but from 1872 to 1887 home to a thriving Chinese community. Fire of suspicious origin destroyed much of the settlement in 1887.

State Capitol site, South Market Street north of Fairmont Hotel between it, and the San Jose Museum of Art, the site where the first California state legislature met in 1849.

U.S. Post Office, now the San Jose Museum of Art, but originally built as a post office in 1892; the city's first federal building.

St. Joseph Cathedral, across West San Fernando Street on South Market Street, north of San Jose Museum of Art, site of the first church of the Pueblo de San Jose.

Juzgado, across South Market Street one block north of St. Joseph Cathedral. The site of the juzgado, or town hall, of the Pueblo de San Jose. Often mispronounced by non-Hispanic settlers as "hoosegow."

Electric Light Tower, intersection of Market and West Santa Clara Streets, where once stood a 237-foot steel tower dotted with electric lights. Erected in 1881 when incandescent bulbs were a new invention, it was designed, in theory, to illuminate the entire downtown area. Although it failed in that goal, it remained in operation until felled by a storm in 1915. (A half-scale replica can be seen at the San Jose Historical Museum.)

San Jose Weekly Visitor, west side of West Santa Clara Street between Market and First Streets, site of the city's first newspaper, published in 1851, and the forerunner of today's *San Jose Mercury News.*

Farmers Union Building, northwest corner of West Santa Clara and San Pedro Streets, once headquarters of the Farmers Union Corporation, established in 1874 as an agricultural cooperative and bank for the valley's farming community.

Lyndon Building, adjacent to Farmers Union Building, built in 1882 and home to a variety of commercial uses ever since.

College of Notre Dame, northeast corner of West Santa Clara St. and Notre Dame Ave., site of California's first chartered women's college, founded in 1851.

Birthplace of A.P. Giannini, west side of North Market Street between West Santa Clara and West St. John Streets, where at 79 North Market St. Amadeo Peter Giannini, founder of the Bank of Italy — now the Bank of America — was born on May 6, 1870.

Thomas Fallon House, north side of West St. John Street between San Pedro and Terraine Streets, home of the Yankee who captained the military seizure of San Jose from Mexican rule and who, in 1859, was elected San Jose's mayor.

Peralta Adobe, across West St. John Street from Fallon House, the oldest Spanish structure downtown and the last physical remnant of the Pueblo de San Jose.

Pellier Park, West St. James Street between San Pedro and Terraine Streets, all that remains of the nursery established in 1850 by Louis Pellier, who brought the French prune to the valley, launching the agricultural industry that dominated San Jose's economy for almost the next 100 years.

Santa Clara County Courthouse, North First Street between St. James and St. John Streets, completed in 1867 in the failed hope of attracting the state legislature back to San Jose.

Post Office, adjacent to courthouse at northwest corner of North First and West St. John Streets, built in 1933 as the city's then-main post office and a prime example of Depression-era federal construction.

Eagles Hall, east side of North Third Street between East St. John and East St. James Streets. Only the Greek Revival facade of this lodge hall, built in 1909, remains today.

First Unitarian Church, adjacent to Eagles Hall on the north and in continuous use by its congregation since 1891.

Scottish Rite Temple, adjacent to First Unitarian Church on the north, completed in 1925 and now the home of the San Jose Athletic Club.

Sainte Claire Club, northeast corner of East St. James and North Second Streets, built in 1893 and home of the city's oldest men's club.

First Church of Christ, Scientist, East St. James between North First and North Second Streets, designed by Willis Polk and built in 1905.

St. James Park, bounded by East St. James, East St. John,

North First and North Second Streets, the heart of 19th Century San Jose and the site of California's last lynching in 1933.

Trinity Episcopal Cathedral, southeast corner of East St. John and North Second Streets, Carpenter Gothic church built in 1863 and the oldest church building in the city.

Labor Temple, 72 North Second St., established between 1901 and 1903 by Harry Ryan, an early San Jose labor leader, and Jack London, the California author.

New Century Block, southeast corner of East Santa Clara and South Second Streets, built in 1880 and a fine example of 19th Century commercial architecture.

Bank of America Building, southeast corner of East Santa Clara and South First Streets, once one of San Jose's earliest skyscrapers and a city landmark since 1926.

Knox-Goodrich Building, south side of South First Street between Santa Clara and San Fernando Streets, typical commercial structure built in 1889.

Letitia Building, adjacent to Knox-Goodrich Building, built in 1890 and named for Letitia Burnett Ryland, daughter of Peter Burnett, the first American civil governor of California.

Bickur Cholim, northeast corner of South Third Street and Paseo de San Antonio, site of San Jose's first Hebrew congregation, founded in 1861.

San Jose Academy, southeast corner of East San Fernando and St. Second Streets, site of a private, non-sectarian preparatory school that held its first graduation ceremony, the first in California, in December, 1851.

Herrold Radio Station, southwest corner of South First and West San Fernando Streets, site of the former Garden City Bank building where radio pioneer Charles Herrold in 1909 became the first person to transmit radio programs of music and news to a listening audience.

5
Climate

Silicon Valley is quintessential California. It boasts an average of more than 300 days of sunshine each year. Typically, the closer you get to San Francisco Bay, the cooler and windier the weather; the farther away, particularly to the east (which also puts you more distant way from the cooling effects of the Pacific Ocean), the warmer.

Using San Jose's central location as a point of reference, the following temperatures offer a general picture:

Avg. Temperature	January	April	July	October	Annual
Daily Maximum:	58	69	81	74	70
Daily Minimum:	41	58	55	51	48
Record High:	79	92	108	97	108
Record Low:	22	32	43	31	20

6
The Lay of the Land

Santa Clara County is one of 58 California counties and the umbrella governmental entity for the valley cradling the southern end of the San Francisco Bay. Within its boundaries, as of the 1990 census, were almost 1.5 million persons, most of them residing in the county's 13 cities. Santa Clara County's major administrative functions are carried on from San Jose, the county seat.

The County Government Center is located at 70 West Hedding St., San Jose 95110. Tel: 408/299-4321.

Campbell, population 34,850, is a central-county residential suburb, mostly middle-income. Its most easily-spotted landmark is the 18-story Pruneyard office tower, adjacent to Highway 17 between Hamilton and Camden Avenues. Median home price range: $255,000–$265,000. City Hall: 70 North First St., Campbell 95008. Tel: 408/866-2100.

Cupertino, population 40,000, is a west valley former bedroom community that in the past two decades has become home to such Silicon Valley industrial giants as Apple and Tandem. Median home price range: $335,000–$355,000. City Hall: 10300 Torre Ave., Cupertino 95014. Tel: 408/252-4505.

Gilroy, population 30,000, is the south county self-proclaimed "Garlic Capital of the World," a boast based on the amount of garlic processed, not grown there. It also has been one of the valley's faster-growing residential areas. Median home price range: $225,000–$240,000. City Hall: 7351 Rosanna St., Gilroy 95020. Tel: 408/842-3191.

Los Altos, population 28,000, is an upscale north county residential community with a village-like downtown commercial area. Median home price: $590,000–$650,000. City Hall: 1 North San Antonio Rd., Los Altos 94022. Tel: 415/948-1491.

Los Altos Hills, population 8,200, is Los Altos' upper income western neighbor, and is exclusively residential. One of the prime addresses for Silicon Valley executives. Median home price range: $980,000–$1,200,000. City Hall: 26379 Fremont Rd., Los Altos Hills 94022. Tel: 415/941-7222.

Los Gatos, population 28,200, is an upscale west valley suburb of expensive homes, with a quaint downtown popular for its variety of restaurants and antique stores. Median home price range: $400,000–$435,000. City Hall: 110 East Main St., Los Gatos 95030. Tel: 408/354-6834.

Milpitas, population 48,100, is an east valley city whose ease of access to many Silicon Valley industrial plants has made it a growing home to an ethnically diverse workforce. Median home price range: $225,000–$240,000. City Hall: 455 East Calaveras Blvd., Milpitas 95035. Tel: 408/942-2310.

Monte Sereno, population 3,500, is the county's smallest city at slightly over one square mile in size and one of its wealthiest. Strictly a bedroom suburb in the west valley hills between Saratoga and Los Gatos. Median home price range: $520,000–$600,000. City Hall: 18041, Saratoga-Los Gatos Rd., Monte Sereno 95030. Tel: 408/354-7635.

Morgan Hill, population 25,000, is the closest southern suburb of San Jose and one of the valley's fastest growing residential areas. It is named for its founder, Morgan Hill, not the smallish peak on its west side, which is called El Toro. Median home price range: $300,000–$335,000. City Hall: 17555 Peak Ave., Morgan Hill 95037. Tel: 408/779-7271.

Mountain View, population 65,000, boasts a north-central county location that has made it a popular choice for both high-tech industrial development and housing. Median home price: $335,000–$355,000. City Hall: 500 Castro St., Mountain View 94041. Tel: 415/903-6300.

Palo Alto, population 58,000, is Silicon Valley's northern-most city, with a bustling downtown, a solid high-tech concentration of corporations and venture capital firms, highly sought-after housing and a focus that historically has ignored anything south of its borders. Home to Stanford University. Median home price: $465,000–$485,000. City Hall: 250 Hamilton Ave., Palo Alto 94301. Tel: 415/329-2571.

San Jose, population 750,000, is the largest city in Northern California and the third largest in the state, whose central-county location and size make it the dominant political entity in Silicon Valley, although some north county cities such as Palo Alto and Los Altos Hills are influenced more by fourth-largest San Francisco. Home to San Jose State University. Median price range: $225,000–$250,000. City Hall: 801 North First St., San Jose 95110. Tel: 408/277-4000.

Santa Clara, population 92,200, borders much-larger San Jose on the north and west but considers itself not a suburb but almost an equal in terms of industrial development, convention facilities and tourism. Home to Santa Clara University. Median home price range: $250,000–$270,000. City Hall: 1500 Warburton Ave., Santa Clara 95050. Tel: 408/984-3000.

Saratoga, population 30,700, is a west valley community with high-priced executive homes in the foothills of the Santa Cruz Mountains and excellent restaurants lining the main street of its small commercial center, Big Basin Way. Median home price range: $625,000–$700,000. City Hall: 13777 Fruit-vale Ave., Saratoga 95070. Tel: 408/867-3438.

Sunnyvale, population 117,300, is the county's second largest city and the home to numerous technology firms, including Lockheed Missiles & Space Co., the county's largest employer. Excellent north-central Silicon Valley location. Median home price: $325,000-$345,000. City Hall: 456 West Olive St., Sunnyvale 94086. Tel: 408/730-7500.

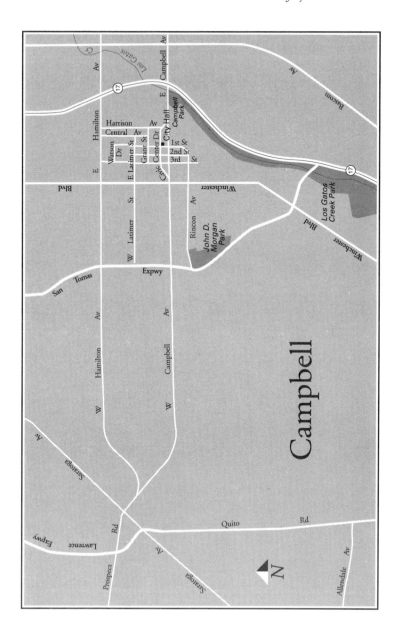

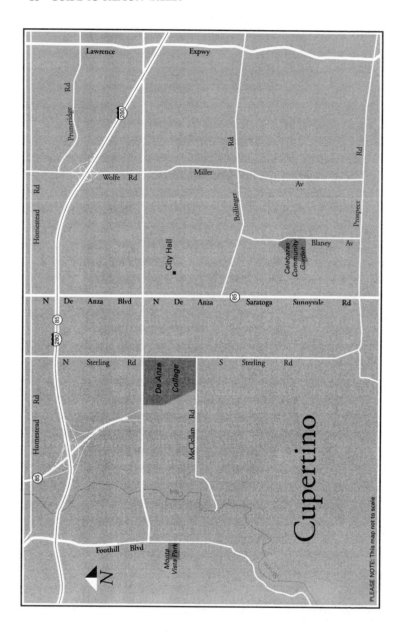

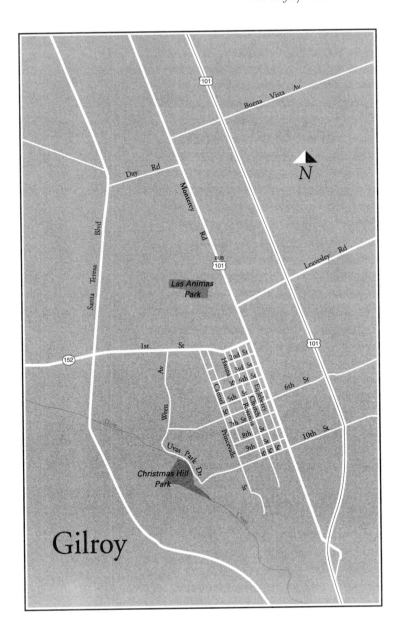

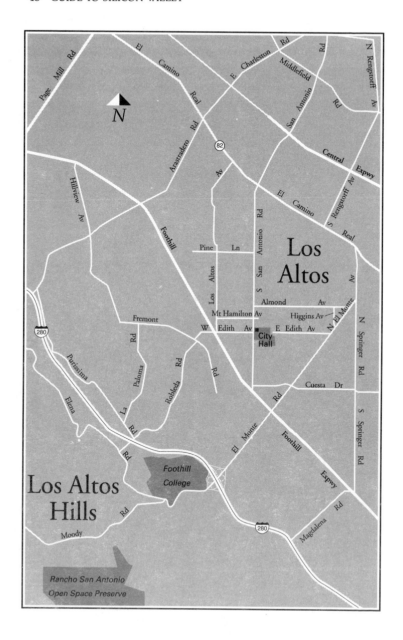

Broadway

84
101

Bayfront Expwy

2nd Av

Fair Oaks

Marsh Rd

84

82

Middlefield

El Camino Real

Glenwood Av

Ravenswood Av

Rd

Willow Rd

84

Menlo Park

Av

Valparaiso Av

Santa Cruz Av

82

Alameda des Las Pulgas

Sand Hill Rd

280

N

Alpine Rd

Junipero Serra Blvd

PLEASE NOTE: This map not to scale

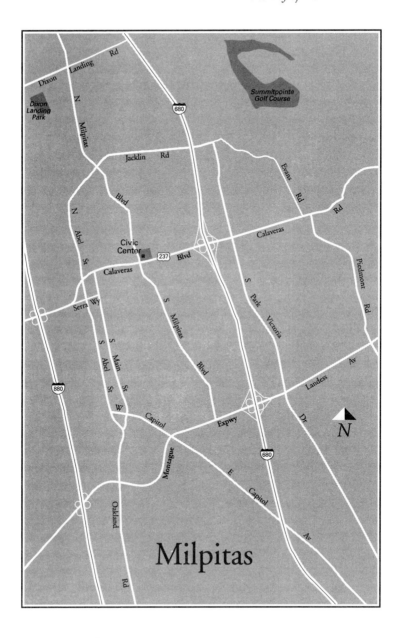

Dixon Landing Rd

Dixon Landing Park

N Milpitas

680

Summitpointe Golf Course

Jacklin Rd

Evans Rd

Blvd

Rd

N Abel St

Calaveras

Civic Center

237 Blvd

Calaveras

S Park Victoria

Piedmont Rd

Serra Wy

S Milpitas

S Main St

S Abel St

Blvd

Landess Av

W

Capitol

Expwy

Dr

N

680

Montague

E Capitol

Av

Oakland

Rd

Milpitas

880

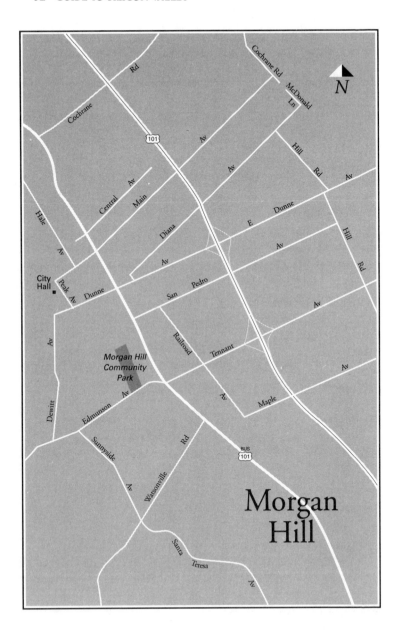

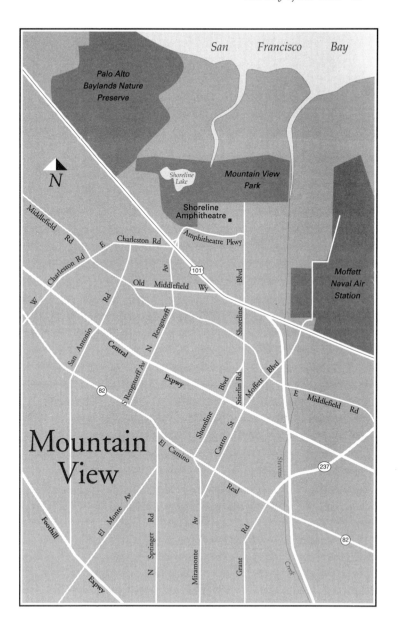

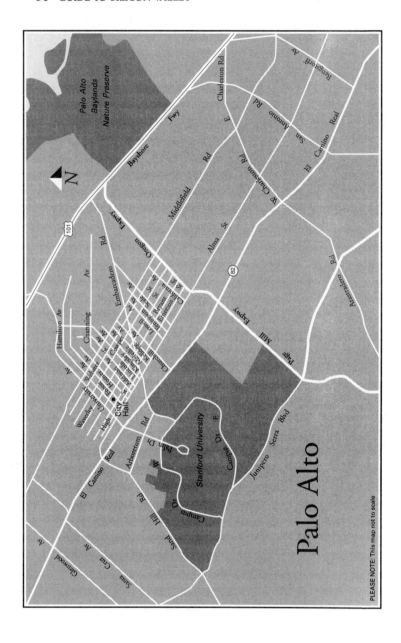

Palo Alto

PLEASE NOTE: This map not to scale

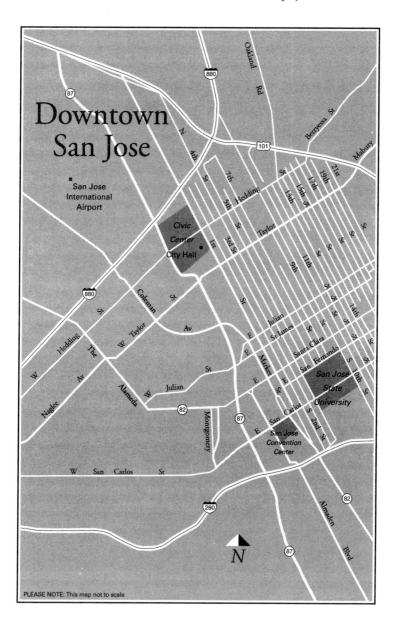

Downtown
San Jose

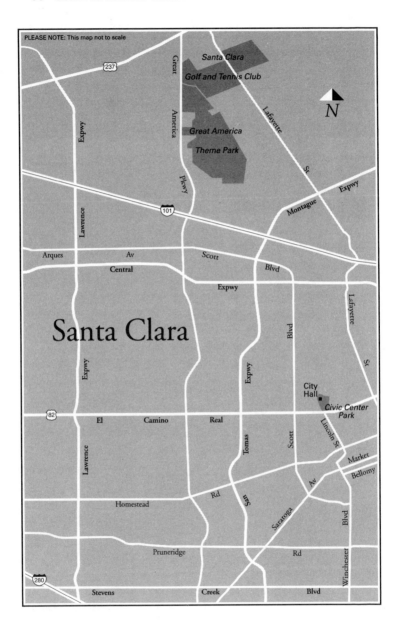

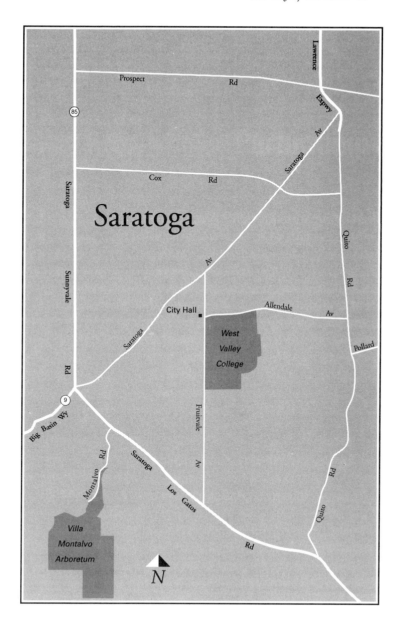

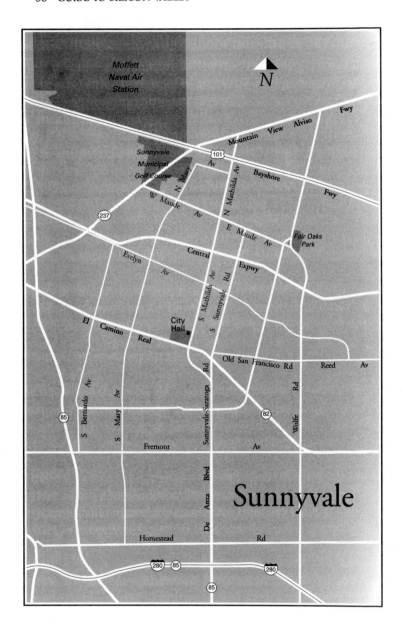

7
Transportation

Getting to Silicon Valley is easy. San Jose International Airport is served by 13 airlines, ranging from international carriers to commuter airlines. Amtrak's West Coast route between Seattle and San Diego stops at the San Jose train depot, and offers connections from there to its intercontinental routes as well. Greyhound Bus Lines serves Silicon Valley with regular stops at San Jose, Sunnyvale and Mountain View. And the region is ringed with freeways, including Interstates 280, 680 and 880, U.S. 101 and State Highway 17.

Getting around Silicon Valley successfully, though, can be more a matter of timing, destination—and luck.

Public transportation is not extensive, by European standards, and the valley's industries, cities and housing are sprawled about, not in one compact cluster. San Jose itself covers more than 250 square miles. Central San Jose is roughly 18 miles from the northernmost Silicon Valley city, Palo Alto, as the crow flies, and crows don't carry passengers.

Some of your choices: If you want to get from central San Jose to, say, Palo Alto, a Caltrain commuter train will do the job. If you are staying in central San Jose and want to traverse no farther than from IBM's main plant in South San Jose to Santa Clara's high-tech, convention and Great America amusement park on the north, then hopping on one of Santa Clara County Transit's light-rail cars will fill the bill. If you want to go east-west, though, or further north to Palo Alto or south to Morgan Hill and Gilroy, then a Santa Clara County Transit bus is your only public option. And if where you want to go is not convenient to any of the bus stops — or if you want the freedom of mobility that puts most Californians behind the wheels of their own cars — then renting or using a car of your own is the best bet. Shorter trips? Take a cab.

All of the above choices have their downsides. Caltrain depots, while connecting the cities of the peninsula between San Jose and San Francisco, aren't always near the high-tech industries or cultural facilities most visitors want to see, and buses don't always connect with the trains' arrival in a timely fashion. The light-rail trolleys, while clean and quick, do not yet extend beyond the valley's central north-south axis. Getting from place to place by bus often requires extensive transfers. Private cars, the valley's most widely used mode of transportation, create major traffic jams. Cabs aren't always waiting for you to flag them down; most often, getting one requires a telephone call.

The details:

Airports

San Jose International Airport, 1661 Airport Blvd., San Jose. Major air carriers, general aviation. General information: 408/277-4759 (call individual airlines for passenger service). Parking information: 408/293-6788.

San Jose Jet Center, 1250 Aviation Ave., San Jose. Facilities at San Jose International Airport for corporate, private jets. Information: 408/297-7552.

Palo Alto Airport, 1925 Embarcadero Road at Palo Alto Yacht Harbor, Palo Alto. Light planes only. Information: 415/856-7833.

Reid-Hillview Airport, 2350 Cunningham Ave., San Jose.

Light planes only. Information: 408/929-2256.

South County Airport, San Martin. Light planes only. Information: 408/683-4741.

Bus

Santa Clara County Transit buses serve all of Santa Clara County from 5 a.m. to 2 a.m. daily. Information: 408/287-4210 for most of the region, 415/965-3100 for Palo Alto and the north county, 408/683-4151 for Morgan Hill, Gilroy and the south county.

Greyhound Lines connects statewide, nationally. Information: San Jose, 408/297-8890. Sunnyvale, 408/737-8287. Mountain View, 415/961-3422.

Rail

Amtrak connects the San Jose depot, 65 Cahill St., with West Coast and intercontinental trains. Information: 408/287-7462, 800/872-7245.

Caltrain stops at 25 stations between San Jose and San Francisco, with 26 trains in each direction on weekdays, 13 on Saturdays and nine on Sundays. Information: 408/287-7462, 800/558-8661.

Santa Clara County Transit operates 50 light-rail vehicles from 5:30 a.m. to 12:30 a.m. between the Santa Clara Convention Center and the IBM plant in South San Jose, plus a half-dozen historical trolleys in a loop through downtown San Jose. Information: 408/287-4210.

Car

Major car rental agencies are represented at San Jose International Airport and at larger cities in Santa Clara County. Limousine service also is available. Consult the local telephone book for individual operators.

Traffic is extremely heavy on Santa Clara County freeways during commute hours (weekdays 6–9 a.m., 4–7 p.m.). Since jobs and housing are not always in the same location, traffic is likely to be heaviest in the northerly and westerly directions during the morning commute, and in the southerly and easterly directions during the evening, although it may not be easy for the driver stuck in bumper-to-bumper traffic to see any difference. At those times and in those directions, using surface streets may be as fast or faster than freeway travel.

Among the major bottlenecks to avoid:
• Afternoon commute southbound on Highway 101 between Lawrence Expressway and Santa Clara Street.
• Afternoon commute southbound on Interstate 280 between Foothill Expressway and Saratoga Avenue.
• Morning commute northbound on Highway 101 between Interstate 280 and Guadalupe Parkway.
• Morning commute northbound on Interstate 280 between Bascom Avenue and Winchester Boulevard.
• Midday automobile travel can be largely free of delays throughout Santa Clara County and often all the way north to San Francisco. Just make certain you limit your driving to between 10 a.m. and 4 p.m. If not, patience—and the knowledge that everyone else probably will be late, too— are advised.

Carpool information and assistance is available from RIDES, 800/755-7665.

8
Speaking Like a Native

If you don't want to sound like a newcomer to Silicon Valley, it helps to know the area's idiosyncracies of pronunciation.

First and foremost, don't call it SiliCONE Valley. Silicone, with an E, is perhaps best known for its use — or misuse — in breast enlargement surgery. The operative word here is SiliCON, which rhymes with Don and Ron and is the prime ingredient in the manufacture of semiconductor chips.

Most of the other pronunciation oddities stem from the valley's Spanish past. Subsequent settlers without practice in speaking Spanish mispronounced at least half of the area's place-names, a situation that continues to this day. The major examples:

Alviso. This former bayside port, now a district of San Jose, still is pronounced the Spanish way: AlVEEso.

Cupertino. A real mixup here. This municipality was named after a city in Italy. Call it KOOPerTEENO or KEWPerTEENO; even the natives can't agree which they prefer.

Los Gatos. Forget the Spanish. Call it Loss GATTus and you'll sound like an old-timer.

Milpitas. Make it MilPEEtas. That's the correct Spanish way, as well as a common opening line for stand-up comedians: "A funny thing happened to me on the way to Milpitas..."

San Jose. Forget those high school Spanish lessons again. It's SannaZAY.

San Martin. Now drag that Spanish primer out again, since this one does follow the rules: San MarTEEN.

It's much the same — mixed up — throughout the rest of the San Francisco Bay Area, as well. A city like San Rafael is Anglicized into San RaFELL while another city, Vallejo, is only semi-Anglicized into VaLAYho. And Diablo, both the mountain and the range it dominates, gets pronounced either English- or Spanish-style — DYEablo or DEEablo — and no one seems to mind. Confused? Don't worry. It's like learning English in the first place — for every rule there's an exception. And besides, so much of the population of Silicon Valley is so relatively new that they're still learning the ins and outs just as you are. Speak without fear. And if the listener looks quizzical or doesn't understand, just try another pronunciation. You'll both understand, eventually.

9
Visual Arts

In a culture largely designed by engineers, where the most important acquisitions are such well-designed adult toys as fast German cars, high-end personal computers and do-everything stereo-video entertainment systems, the more quirky sorts of pleasures such as the visual arts are only now starting to come into their own. Where before home-grown artists would have to head for larger metropolitan areas to make a living, Silicon Valley in the 1990s now has a sufficiently large and well-educated population to begin supporting the variously artistically creative individuals in its midst. Engineers themselves are starting to go beyond buying Neiman lithographs at the malls and are seeking out non-mass-produced artworks instead. Corporations, most notably Syntex, support and nurture area artists through acquisitions and on-site gallery shows. Developers grace the lobbies of their buildings with Louise Nevelson and Benny Bufano statuary. San Jose State University's art department, which for years turned out artists of stature and then saw them depart for other locales, has become a home base for local talent.

The best places to view art:

Museums

American Museum of Quilts and Textiles. As the name indicates, quilts, from traditional to modern, are the specialty here. 766 South Second St., San Jose. Tel: 408/971-0323. Hours: 10 a.m.–4 p.m., Tuesday–Saturday.

de Saisset Museum. Fare ranges from local artists to touring national exhibits, often on ethical or moral issues. Permanent collection leans toward the traditional. Santa Clara University, The Alameda and Franklin St., Santa Clara. Tel: 408/554-4528. Hours: 11 a.m.–4 p.m., Tuesday–Sunday. Guided tours by appointment.

Euphrat Museum of Art. Specializes in contemporary works by Silicon Valley and Bay Area artists. De Anza College, 21250 Stevens Creek Blvd., Cupertino. Tel: 408/864-8836. Hours: 11 a.m.–4 p.m., Tuesday–Thursday; 6–8 p.m. Wednesday; 11–2, Saturday.

Egyptian Museum and Planetarium. Part of the world headquarters of the Rosicrucian Order, it has a large collection of Egyptian and Mideast artifacts, including mummies and a reconstruction of a noble's burial tomb. Additional displays include modern artwork by local artists, a science center and a planetarium. Park and Naglee Avenues, San Jose. Tel: 408/287-2807. Hours: 9 a.m.–5 p.m., daily.

San Jose Museum of Art. Silicon Valley's largest museum, mounting both locally curated shows and hosting touring national exhibitions. Private collection emphasizes works of the 20th Century. 110 South Market St., San Jose. Tel: 408/294-2787. Hours: 10 a.m.–6 p.m., Tuesday–Friday; 10 a.m.–4 p.m., Saturday; noon–4 p.m., Sunday.

Stanford Museum of Art. The museum is currently closed indefinitely because of damage suffered in the 1989 earthquake, but adjacent Rodin sculpture garden features a stunning collection of the French master's bronzes. Museum Way, Stanford University, Palo Alto. Tel: 415/723-3469. Garden tours: 2 p.m., Wednesdays, Saturdays and Sundays.

Triton Museum of Art. Intelligently curated local exhibits, some touring shows. Permanent collection emphasizes

California artists. 1505 Warburton Ave., Santa Clara. Tel: 408/247-3754. Hours: 10 a.m.–5 p.m., Monday through Friday, except Wednesday open until 9 p.m.; noon–5 p.m., weekends.

Leading Galleries

Bingham Gallery, Fairmont Hotel, 170 South Market St., San Jose. Tel: 408/993-1066.

Citadel Print Center, 199 Martha St. #23, San Jose. Tel: 408/289-9316.

Frederick Spratt Gallery, 920 South First St., San Jose. Tel: 408/294-1135.

Holmes Fine Art, 97 South Second St., San Jose. Tel: 408/971-9100.

Palo Alto Cultural Center, 1313 Newell Rd., Palo Alto. Tel: 415/329-2366.

San Jose Art League, 14 South First St., San Jose. Tel: 408/287-8435.

San Jose Institute of Contemporary Art, 2 North Second St., San Jose. Tel: 408/998-4310.

San Jose State University Galleries, San Jose State University, South Fourth and San Fernando Sts., San Jose. Tel: 408/924-4320.

Smith Anderson Gallery, 200 Homer St., Palo Alto. Tel: 415/327-7762.

Stanford Art Gallery, Stanford University near Hoover Tower, Palo Alto. Tel: 415/723-2842.

Villa Montalvo Gallery, Villa Montalvo Center for the Arts, 15400 Montalvo Rd., Saratoga. Tel: 408/741-3421.

Works/San Jose, 260 Jackson St., San Jose. Tel: 408/295-8378.

Young Gallery, 307 North Santa Cruz Ave., Los Gatos. Tel: 408/399-1900.

10
Performing Arts

Silicon Valley's performing arts picture is, for the most part, as new as the valley's technological and population growth. Overshadowed for years by the cultural organizations and facilities of San Francisco, it only recently began to come into its own, albeit still in a catch-up position relative to its now smaller neighbor to the north. All the main components of the performing arts spectrum are in place, however, and the valley's professional and semi-professional arts organizations are bulwarked by extensive amateur and little-theater participation so that growth in this area seems assured.

Among the major players:

Dance

San Jose Cleveland Ballet, a joint venture between the two cities, with the dancers splitting performance time between both. Ranked among the nation's top regional ballet companies. Box 1666, San Jose. Tel: 408/288-2800.

San Jose Dance Theater, tel: 408/293-5665; **Santa Clara Ballet,** tel: 408/247-9178; and **Western Ballet,** tel: 415/948-5696, are associated with pre-professional training academies.

Margaret Wingrove Dance Company of San Jose, tel: 408/867-0475, and **Janlyn Dance Company of Cupertino,** tel: 408/255-4055, present modern dance works.

Ethnic Performance

The valley's ethnically diverse population is well represented in the performing arts with a variety of troupes —from professional to amateur—representing the spectrum of artistic endeavor. These include:

Abhinaya Dance Company, a folkloric dance group offering performances and classes in the classical dance of India. 476 Park Ave., Suite 226, San Jose 95110, tel: 408/993-9231.

Los Lupenos de San Jose, a folkloric dance group featuring traditional dances of Mexico. P.O. Box 997, 40 North First St., San Jose 95108, tel: 408/292-0443.

San Jose Flamenco Society, dedicated to the traditional Spanish guitar and dance form., P.O.Box 7173, San Jose 95150, tel: 408/723-0354.

San Jose Taiko Group, specializing in Japanese drumming, often with intricately choreographed movements and dramatic staging, which in two decades of performing has gone from amateur to professional. P.O. Box 26895, San Jose 95159, tel: 408/293-9344.

Musical Comedy

San Jose Civic Light Opera, the nation's largest subscription musical theater, performs a full season of Broadway musicals. Tel: 408/453-7100.

Opera

Opera San Jose, founded by former Metropolitan Opera performer Irene Dalis, performs fully staged operas with resident–artists and trainees. Tel: 408/288-7077.

Symphony

Palo Alto Chamber Orchestra, a chamber orchestra with a performing record of more than a quarter–century. Tel: 415/856-3848.

San Jose Symphony, with Leonid Grin as music director, is more than a century old and has been performing longer than any other symphony in the western United States. Tel: 408/288-2828.

San Jose Chamber Orchestra, directed by Barbara Day Turner, specializes in chamber repertoire. Tel: 408/286-5111.

Theater

California Theater Center, Sunnyvale Repertory Company, a semi-professional troupe featuring a regular summer schedule of performances at the Sunnyvale Performing Arts Center. Other performances as announced. Tel: 408/245-2978.

City Lights Theater Company, a semi-professional theatrical troupe specializing in avant-garde or new works. Tel: 408/295-4200.

San Jose Repertory Theatre, a fully professional, Equity company, offers a full season of drama from classic to contemporary. Tel: 408/291-2255.

San Jose Stage Company is a semi-professional theater company specializing in contemporary works. Tel: 408/283-7142

TheatreWorks of Palo Alto, a semi-professional company that nevertheless produces works of considerable quality, especially modern musicals. Tel: 415/323-8311.

Where They Perform

Since Silicon Valley grew faster in commerce and population than in the arts, performance space is at a premium. A number of the preceding organizations must share stage space while they plan for permanent homes of their own.

To find out who is performing where and when, it is advisable to contact the performance groups directly. For box office information about performances at city-sponsored venues in San Jose, a hotline is available at 408/288-7469. Or, you may contact the venues themselves for performance information about local companies and touring shows. Silicon Valley's major sites are:

Flint Center, at De Anza College, 21250 Stevens Creek Blvd., Cupertino. Tel: 408/864-8816.

Mountain View Center for the Performing Arts, Mercy and Castro Streets, Mountain View. Tel: 415/903-6000.

The Mountain Winery, 14831 Pierce Rd., Saratoga. Tel: 408/741-5183.

Montgomery Theater, South Market St. at West San Carlos St., San Jose. Tel: 408/277-3900.

San Jose Arena, West Santa Clara St. at Montgomery St. Tel: 408/287-9200.

San Jose Center for the Performing Arts, Almaden Boulevard at Park Avenue, San Jose. Tel: 408/277-3900; 800/533-2345.

San Jose Civic Auditorium, 145 West San Carlos St., San Jose. Tel: 408/277-3900.

San Jose State University Event Center, South Seventh Street near the SJSU campus's south side. Tel: 408/924-3267.

Shoreline Amphitheater, 1 Amphitheater Parkway, Mountain View. Tel: 415/967-3000.

Lucie Stern Theater, 1305 Middlefield Rd., Palo Alto. Tel: 415/329-2623.

Villa Montalvo Center for the Arts, 15400 Montalvo Rd., Saratoga. Tel: 408/741-3421.

11
Dining

What kind of dining do you seek? Be advised that this is multi-cultural California, where virtually all examples of ethnic cuisine are available. Also be advised that since this is California, diners are willing to drive 20 miles or more just to find the particular dishes they desire on a particular day; this can be serious territory for serious food fans.

Restaurants are coded in this book by cost and credit card acceptance as follows:

$ = most entrees are under $10
$$ = entrees range from $10 to $20
$$$ = most entrees are more than $20

Credit cards accepted:
AE = American Express   D = Discover
CB = Carte Blanche   MC = Mastercard
DC = Diners Club   V = Visa

A Gourmet's Top Ten

Longtime Silicon Valley restaurant critic and author Joseph Izzo Jr. offers this quick sampler of restaurants where satisfaction should be guaranteed:

Adriatic. A setting of Old World charm, complete with quiet, intimate tables and expert, continental fare, leaning as the name indicates, toward Eastern European. 14583 Big Basin Way, Saratoga. Reservations required. Tel: 408/867-3110. $$ AE, CB, D, DC, MC, V.

Birk's. The pleasures of the American grill and smokehouse in a stunning package of stylish decor; a particular favorite of San Francisco 49er football players, who train nearby. 3955 Freedom Circle, Santa Clara. Reservations required for lunch, suggested for dinner. Tel: 408/980-6400. $$ AE, CB, DC, MC, V.

Campbell House. Delicious French/California specialties served in a converted California bungalow that offers a warm dining space of unpretentious design. 106 East Campbell Ave., Campbell. Reservations suggested. Tel: 408/374-5757. $$ AE, CB, DC, MC, V.

Chez T.J. French specialties, emphasizing fresh California produce, served in a homelike, candlelit setting with quiet elegance. 938 Villa St., Mountain View. Reservations suggested. Tel: 415/964-7466. $$$ MC, V.

Emile's. Nothing less than unparalleled dining from the cuisine minceur repertoire of San Jose's most celebrated chef, Emile Mooser. 545 South Second St., San Jose. Reservations suggested. Tel: 408/289-1960. $$ AE, CB, DC, MC, V.

Fung Lum. An ornately decorated temple to the Hong Kong style of Chinese cuisine. 1815 South Bascom Ave., Campbell. Tel: 408/377-6955. $$ AE, CB, D, DC, MC, V.

La Mere Michelle. Soft light, handsome furnishings, exquisite food derived from classic European recipes. 14467 Big Basin Way, Saratoga. Tel: 408/867-5272. $$ AE, CB, DC, MC, V.

La Foret. A fail-safe for "occasion" continental dining in a secluded, creekside setting in the historic New Almaden district. 21747 Bertram Rd., San Jose. Tel: 408/997-3458. $$$ AE, CB, DC, MC, V.

Le Mouton Noir. Country French, with warm ambiance and impeccable service. 14560 Big Basin Way, Saratoga. Tel: 408/867-7017. $$ AE, CB, DC, MC, V.

Paolo's. San Jose's granddaddy of fine Italian dining in a modern new setting where traditional values and inventive Italian cooking make compelling harmony. 333 West San Carlos St., San Jose. Reservations suggested. Tel: 408/294-2558. $$ AE, CB, D, DC, MC, V.

The Best of the Rest

AMERICAN/CALIFORNIA CUISINE

California Cafe. Fresh local produce, imaginative entrees. Four locations throughout Silicon Valley: 2855 Stevens Creek Blvd., San Jose, tel: 408/244-1556; 50 University Ave., Los Gatos, tel: 408/354-8118; 5925 Almaden Expy, Almaden Valley, tel:408/268-2233; and 855 East Homestead Rd., San Jose, tel:408/739-7670. Non-smoking. $$ AE, CB, DC, MC, V.

840 North First. Contemporary cuisine with obligatory side orders of political talk; it's the closest white-tablecloth restaurant to the San Jose Civic Center, the nexus of Silicon Valley political life. 840 North First St., San Jose. Reservations suggested. Tel: 408/282-0840. $$ AE, CB, DC, MC, V.

Eulipia. Seasonally changing menu, contemporary creativity, and still a major gathering place for San Jose's movers and shakers. 374 South First St., San Jose. Reservations suggested. Tel: 408/280-6161. $$ AE, MC, V.

Flea Street Cafe. Pays special attention to fresh, local produce. 3607 Alameda de las Pulgas, Menlo Park. Tel: 415/854-1226. $$ MC, V.

Fresh Choice. Emphasis on fresh produce, extensive luncheon menu for the health-conscious. Nine locations in Silicon Valley: 5353 Almaden Expressway, San Jose, tel: 408/723-7991;

1600 Saratoga Ave., San Jose, tel: 408/866-1491; 555 East Calaveras Blvd., Milpitas, tel: 408/262-6604; 3041 Stevens Creek Blvd., Santa Clara, tel: 408/243-7402; 1654 South Bascom Ave., Campbell, tel: 408/559-1912; 10123 North Wolfe Rd., Cupertino, tel: 408/253-1605; 180 El Camino Real, Palo Alto, tel: 415/322-6995; 1105 West El Camino Real, Sunnyvale, tel: 408/732-7788; 333 Moffett Park Dr., Sunnyvale, tel: 408/734-0661. $ MC, V.

Garden City. American steak and chop house, plus jazz music and, in the bulk of its building, San Jose's largest card room (poker, lo-ball, pan, most legal California gambling games). 360 South Saratoga Ave., San Jose. Tel: 408/244-3333. $$ AE, CB, DC, MC, V.

Good Earth. Quintessential California health-food restaurants. Four locations in Silicon Valley: 20807 Stevens Creek Blvd., Cupertino, tel: 408/252-3555; 206 North Santa Cruz Ave., Los Gatos, tel: 408/395-6868; 2705 The Alameda, Santa Clara, tel: 408/984-0960; 185 University Ave., Palo Alto, tel: 415/321-9449. $ AE, DC, MC, V.

Gordon Biersch. Beer brewed on the premises to accompany casual menu of thirst-inducing appetizers, entrees. Reservations suggested. 33 East San Fernando St., San Jose, tel: 408/294-6785; and 640 Emerson St., Palo Alto, tel: 415/323-7723. $$ AE, CB, DC, MC, V.

Lion & Compass. All the California cuisine combinations, given a Silicon Valley power-dining twist by founder Nolan Bushnell, the inventor of Pong and other high-tech sports. 1023 North Fair Oaks Ave., Sunnyvale. Tel: 408/745-1260. $$ AE, CB, DC, MC, V.

MacArthur Park. Mesquite-grilled meats, fish; famous ribs. 27 University Ave., Palo Alto. Tel: 415/321-9990. $$ AE, MC, V.

Tied House. Excellent, brewed-on-the-premises beer and appropriate pub food. 65 North San Pedro St., San Jose, tel: 408/295-2739; and 954 Villa St., Mountain View, tel: 415/

965-2739. $$ AE, CB, DC, MC, V.

AFGHAN

Kabul. Charcoal-broiled, marinated lamb is the specialty. 135 El Camino Real, Santa Clara. Tel: 408/594-2840. $$ MC, V.

AUSTRALIAN

Aussie's. The premises look fast-food but the menu is Down Under; meat pies, Aussie soul food. 1187 South Saratoga-Sunnyvale Rd., San Jose. Tel: 408/466-3170. $ Cash/checks.

Australian Restaurant. Casual cafe featuring Aussie tucker. 898 Lincoln Ave., San Jose. Tel: 408/293-1112. $ Cash/checks.

BARBECUE

Ernie the Butcher. Basic barbecue for meat-eaters in ultra-casual, strip commercial setting. 1404 South Bascom Ave., San Jose. Tel: 408/995-6232. $ MC, V.

Goldie's Oakwood Bar-B-Que. An oasis of ribs, chicken and hot links in a downtown setting. 21 North Second St., San Jose. Tel: 408/279-2720. $ MC, V.

Henry's Hi-Life. Saloon/steakhouse setting with menu to match. 301 West St. John St., San Jose. Tel: 408/295-5414. $$ DC, MC, V.

Quincy's. Down home soul food, the real article. 70 North Main St., Milpitas. Tel: 408/945-7943. $, Cash/checks.

BRITISH

Brittania Arms. All the expected pub specialties; a particular home away from home for expatriate soccer (football) fans. 5027 Almaden Expressway, San Jose, tel: 408/266-0550; and

1087 South Sunnyvale-Saratoga Rd., Cupertino, tel: 408/252-7262. $ AE, MC, V.

Welshman's Arms. Standard pub specialties. 693 Grape Ave., Sunnyvale. Tel: 408/736-9199. $ AE, MC, V.

CAJUN

Louisiana Territory. Louisiana oysters are flown in; andouille makes the trip, too. 2290 West El Camino Real, Mountain View. Reservations suggested. Tel: 415/964-8900. $$ AE, DC, MC, V.

Old Alligator Grill. Home-style Louisiana cooking, with all the regulars: catfish, shrimp, jambalaya. 15 1/2 North Santa Cruz Ave., Los Gatos. Tel: 408/395-7339. $ MC, V.

CAMBODIAN

Chez Sovan. Very little ambiance, but excellent Cambodian food at reasonable prices more than makes up for it. 923 Old Oakland Rd., San Jose. Tel: 408/287-7619. $ AE, CB, DC, MC, V.

CARIBBEAN

Mango Cafe. Jerk chicken and pork (that's barbecue, Jamaica and Trinidad style), lots of tropical fruit. 483 University Ave., Palo Alto. Tel: 415/325-3229. $ Cash/checks.

CHINESE

Chef Chu's. Mandarin cuisine from a well-established favorite. 1067 North San Antonio Rd., Los Altos. Tel: 415/948-2696. $ AE, CB, DC, MC, V.

Golden Wok. Szechuan and Mandarin specialties. (Nearby Castro Street also offers a wide variety of excellent Oriental restaurants for those willing to walk for variety). 895 Villa St., Mountain View. Tel: 415/969-8232. $ AE, MC, V.

Pagoda. Elegant surroundings, Cantonese/Kwangtung/ Szechuan specialties. Fairmont Hotel, 170 South Market St., San Jose. Reservations suggested. Tel: 998-3937. $$ AE, CB, DC, MC, V.

CONTINENTAL

Dartanian's. Another hideaway, this in a neighborhood shopping center. Continental with Italian leanings. 1655 South Saratoga-Sunnyvale Rd., Cupertino. Tel: 408/257-1120. $$ AE, MC, V.

Les Saisons. Elegantly formal continental fare with California accents. Excellent wine list. Fairmont Hotel, 170 South Market St., San Jose. Reservations suggested. Tel: 408/998-3950. $$$ AE, CB, DC, MC, V.

The Plumed Horse. Elegant, with a nod toward the French. One of the valley's most extensive wine lists. 14555 Big Basin Way, Saratoga. Reservations suggested. Tel: 408/867-4711. $$$ AE, MC, V.

EAST-WEST

Chez Nous Hama. Take your pick from the Japanese menu or the French menu, or mix and match. 20030 Stevens Creek Blvd., Cupertino. Tel: 408/446- 4262. $$ AE, DC, MC, V.

Gerard's. Predominantly French but with Asian creativity; offers dinner packages with performances at adjoining Club Jazz, plus in-house live jazz performances for dinner hour and Sunday brunch. 55 South Market St., San Jose. Reservations suggested on weekends. Tel: 408/279-8110. $ AE, MC, V.

Martha's. Pacific Rim dining with influences from California to China in simple, elegant surroundings. 1875 South Bascom Ave., Campbell. Reservations suggested. Tel: 408/ 377-1193. $$ MC, V.

ETHIOPIAN

Horn of Africa. Ethiopian/East African cuisine in casual surroundings. 17 East Santa Clara St., San Jose. Tel: 408/283-0822. $ MC, V.

Red Sea. Spicy, authentic Ethiopian fare, with Italian asides. 684 North First St., San Jose. Tel: 408/993-1990. $ MC, V.

FRENCH

Beausejour. Impeccable presentation, with cuisine to match. 170 State St., Los Altos. Tel: 415/948-1382. $$ AE, MC, V.

Gervais. Chef Gervais Henric proves that traditional French cuisine can succeed even in a neighborhood shopping center setting. 1798 Park Ave., San Jose. Tel: 408/275-8631. $$ AE, DC, MC, V.

L'Horizon. Overlooking San Jose International Airport at the San Jose Jet Center. The place for fine French fare while you're getting your private jet refueled. 1250 Aviation Ave., San Jose. Tel: 408/295-1771. $$ AE, MC, V.

Le Papillon. Favored for those discreet meals where a low profile is as important as haute cuisine. 410 Saratoga Ave., San Jose. Tel: 408/296-3730. $$$ AE, CB, DC, MC, V.

Rue de Paris. Intimate French cafe setting, classic cuisine. 19 North Market St., San Jose. Tel: 408/298-0704. $$ AE, CB, DC, MC, V.

GERMAN

Gasthaus zum Goldenen Adler. Traditional fare, with emphasis on game. 1380 South Main St., Milpitas. Tel: 408/946-6141. $ AE, MC, V.

Hardy's. Game specialties, homemade sauerkraut. 111 West Evelyn Ave., Sunnyvale. Tel: 408/720-1531. $ AE, MC, V.

Hochburg von Germania. Traditional fare in historic meeting hall for valley's early German residents. 261 North Second St., San Jose. Tel: 408/295- 4484. $$ AE, DC, MC, V.

Teske's Germania. Traditional fare, plus pleasant outdoor beer garden. 255 North First St., San Jose. Tel: 408/292-0291. $$ AE, MC, V.

GREEK

Zorba. Lemon-chicken soup, stuffed grape leaves, moussaka, all the classics. 1350 South Bascom Ave., San Jose. Tel: 408/293-7170. $$ AE, MC, V.

INDIAN

Mumtaj. Northern Indian specialties, tandoor oven. 126 Castro St., Mountain View. Tel: 415/961-2433. $$ AE, MC, V.

Vindu. Especially flavorful curries. 1146 Saratoga-Sunnyvale Rd., Cupertino. Tel: 408/446-3390. $$ AE, MC, V.

ITALIAN

Bellino. Modern Italian, featuring wood-burning oven and grill for pizzas, meat, fish and fowl. Terraces overlooking St. Joseph Cathedral, San Jose Museum of Art. 95 South Market St., San Jose. Tel: 408/277-0690. $$ AE, MC, V.

Cafe Marcella. An attractive cafe, light and airy, serving first-class bistro fare. 368 Village Lane, Los Gatos. Tel: 408/354-8006. $$ MC, V.

Fontana's. Italian staples, California-influenced. And it has its own bocce court. 20840 Stevens Creek Blvd., Cupertino. Tel: 408/725-0188. $$ AE, MC, V.

Il Fornaio. Spectacular decor, cuisine to match. Outstanding bread. Sainte Claire Hotel, Market and San Carlos Streets, San Jose, tel: 408/271-3366; and 520 Cowper St., Palo Alto, tel: 415/853-3888. $$$ MC, V.

La Pastaia. The former is friendly and noisy with a big exhibition kitchen, the latter a quieter cafe, with both featuring such Italian comfort foods as polenta and a variety of pastas. De Anza Hotel, 233 West Santa Clara St., San Jose, tel: 408/286-8686; and 420 Emerson St., Palo Alto, tel: 415/323-2464. $$ AE, MC, V.

Margherita di Roma. Roman-style favorites, homey atmosphere. 14482 Big Basin Way, Saratoga. tel: 408/867-9178. $$ AE, MC, V.

Original Joe's. No nonsense Italian fare, huge portions, entertaining exhibition kitchen. 301 South First St., San Jose. Tel: 292-7030. $ MC, V.

Palermo. Sicilian down-home cooking, like Grandma should have made. The Palo Alto branch features rotisserie dishes. 394 South Second St., San Jose, tel: 297-0607; and 452 University Ave., Palo Alto, tel: 415/494-0700. $$ MC, V.

Pasquale's. Mostly Southern Italian classics; exceptionally pleasant patio dining for alfresco fans. 476 South First St., San Jose. Tel: 286-1770. $$ AE, CB, DC, MC, V.

Sal and Luigi Pizzeria. Okay pizza, but they make their own gnocchi and ravioli. Major meatballs, too. 347 South First St., San Jose. Tel: 408/297-1136. $ Cash only.

JAPANESE

California Sushi and Grill. Sushi, of course, with a grill that also turns out teriyaki specialties, and uncommon items such as hamachi cheeks. 1 East San Fernando St., San Jose. Tel: 408/297-1847. $ AE, MC, V.

Ikenohana. Elegant dining, impeccable service and exquisite preparation of classic Japanese cuisine. 20625 Alves

Dr., Cupertino. Tel: 408/252-6460. $$ AE, MC, V.

Fuki-Sushi. Wide range of Japanese cuisine, including sushi, teriyaki, tempura, sashimi. Appetizers to complete dinners. 4119 El Camino Real, Palo Alto. Tel: 415/494-9383. $$ AE, MC, V.

House of Genji. Teppan-style cooking, as popularized in the United States by Benihana. 1335 North First St., San Jose. Tel: 408/453-8120. $ AE, MC, V.

Sono Sushi. Classic Japanese sushi bar with floating sushi boats from which diners can select their favorites as they drift by. 357 Castro St., Mountain View. Tel: 415/961-9086. $ MC, V.

KOREAN

Korean Palace. Bulgogi, kim chee, other traditional Korean favorites. 2297 Stevens Creek Blvd., San Jose. Tel: 408/947-8600. $ AE, MC, V.

MEXICAN

Andale. Mesquite-grilled meat and fowl, bountiful burritos. Three locations: 21 North Santa Cruz Ave., Los Gatos, tel: 408/395-8997; 6 North Santa Cruz Ave., Los Gatos, tel: 408/395-4244; and 209 University Ave., Palo Alto, tel: 415/323-2939. $ Cash/checks.

Baja Cactus. Homemade Mexican specialties, including goat, carne adobado. 338 South Main St., Milpitas. Tel: 408/263-9455. $ DC, MC, V.

Casa Castillo. Exceptional tamales; pleasant sidewalk cafe dining, weather permitting. 200 South First St., San Jose. Tel: 408/971-8130. $ MC, V.

Pedro's. Originator and best example of the regional chain by same name; Mexican food tamed for Yanqui tastes. 316 North Santa Cruz Ave., Los Gatos. Tel: 408/354-7570. $ MC, V.

Sinaloa. Authentic Mexican roadhouse in both atmosphere, cuisine. 19210 Monterey Rd., Morgan Hill. Tel: 408/779-9740. $ Cash/checks.

MOROCCAN

El Maghreb. Low tables, cushions, traditional fare to be eaten out of hand, plus belly dancers. 145 West Santa Clara St., San Jose. Tel: 408/294-2243. $ AE, MC, V.

Menara. Lemon chicken, lamb with honey, b'stilla, couscous, mint tea. The works, and belly dancers. Friday lunch only, dinners nightly. 41 East Gish Rd., San Jose. Tel: 408/453-1983. $ AE, MC, V.

POLISH

Eugene's. Standards, including goulash, bigos and pierogi. 420 South San Antonio Rd., Los Altos. Tel: 415/941-1222. $$ MC, V, checks.

PORTUGUESE

Tamar. Emphasis on cod, other typical country fare. 1610 and 1612 Alum Rock Ave., San Jose. Tel: 408/258-5656. $$ MC, V.

SALVADORAN

El Calderon. Traditional pork- or bean-filled pupusas, other national specialties. 699 Calderon Ave., Mountain View. Tel: 415/940-9533. $ Cash/checks.

SPANISH

Iberia. Extensive menu, long wine list, dining both indoors and out. 190 Ladera-Alpine Rd., Portola Valley. Tel: 415/854-1746. $$ AE, MC, V.

SEAFOOD

Fish Market. They'll sell you fish to take home or cook it for you there. Long-time favorite. 3775 El Camino Real, Santa Clara, tel: 408/246-3474; and 3150 El Camino Real, Palo Alto, tel: 415/493-9188. $$ AE, CB, DC, MC, V.

Mariscos Inda. The Mexican way with fish, oysters, chowders. 205 North Fourth St., San Jose, tel: 408/297-5598; and 300 Willow, San Jose. $ Cash.

Pacific Fresh. The name says it; large selection of fresh seafood. 21255 Stevens Creek Blvd., Cupertino, tel: 408/252-5311; and 1130 North Mathilda Ave., Sunnyvale, tel: 408/745-1710. $$ AE, CB, DC, MC, V.

Scott's. Penthouse setting, scrupulously fresh seafood. Favorite for downtown San Jose power-lunching, but complementary lighting makes it romantic for dinner. 185 Park Ave., San Jose. Reservations suggested. Tel: 408/971-1700. $$ AE, MC, V.

Steamer's. Oyster bar, grill and saute specialties including calamari della casa (squid with capers and wine). 50 University Ave., Los Gatos. Tel: 408/395-2722. $$ MC, V.

THAI

High-Thai. Palate-tingling traditional Thai cuisine. 335 Saratoga Ave., San Jose. Tel: 408/248-8813. $ AE, MC, V.

Krung Thai. Basic Thai fare, reasonable prices. 1699 West San Carlos Blvd., San Jose. Tel: 408/295-5508. $ MC, V.

VIETNAMESE

Golden Chopsticks. Stylish restaurant, with full range of Vietnamese specialties, French emphasis. 1765 South Winchester Blvd., Campbell. Reservations suggested. Tel: 408/370-6610. $ AE, D, DC, MC, V.

Quoc Te. One of the longest Vietnamese menus in the valley. Excellent firepot dishes. Open late for after-theater dining. 155 East San Fernando St., San Jose. Tel: 408/289-8323. $ MC, V.

Thanh Hien. Shopping center setting, but a great place for pho, the traditional Vietnamese soup. 2345 McKee Rd., San Jose. Tel: 408/926-1056. $ MC, V over $20.

12
Nightlife

Silicon Valley's popular entertainment options run the gamut, from central city jazz clubs to hilltop amphitheaters, from major artists performing in large arena settings to up-and-coming hopefuls in small, suburban shopping center venues. With the exception of downtown San Jose, where a variety of clubs and performance halls are clustered, there is little chance for pub-crawling on foot. But this is California, after all, where wheels are king and residents think nothing of driving 20 or 30 miles in an evening if the attraction is great enough. Get a car, if you need to, and join them.

David Plotnikoff, who covers the nightlife scene for the *San Jose Mercury News,* offers this Top 10 list of venues for your pleasure:

The Mountain Winery, 14831 Pierce Rd., Saratoga. Tel: 408/741-0763. Far and away the most spectacular outdoor setting for pop music in the valley. Breathtaking views, gracious staff and more than 100 top-flight shows each year.

F/X, 400 South First St., San Jose. Tel: 408/298-9796. The top downtown haunt for young artists, hip college students and alternative-rock aficionados. The remodeled movie theater features everything from dance revues and local rock to hardcore hip-hop disc jockeys. Go late (after 11 p.m.) to catch the dance-floor scene in full swing. Cover usually ranges from $3 to $6.

The Saddle Rack, 1310 Auzerais Ave., San Jose. Tel: 408/286-3393. This vast wonderland of countrified pleasures is so large it has its own neighborhoods. Two stages, three dance floors and five bars. Usually no cover, except for shows by national country-western headliners.

The Garden City, 360 South Saratoga Ave., San Jose. Tel: 408/244-3333. San Jose's answer to South Lake Tahoe's casino scene. This cathedral-like club features poker 24 hours a day and an outstanding restaurant with live jazz nightly. A real class act.

The Ajax Lounge, 374 South First St., San Jose. Tel: 408/298-2529. The hot downtown scene's drawing room — great for conversation and light jazz after dinner downstairs at the Eulipia restaurant or a film next door at the Camera One Cinema. Cover varies.

The Cactus Club, 417 South First St., San Jose. Tel: 408/280-1435. Hard-rock heaven on most nights, with national alternative rock and disc jockey dancing to round out the slate. You say you don't have a black leather biker jacket? Get one, dude. 18 and over. Cover varies.

Toons, 52 East Santa Clara St., San Jose. Tel: 408/292-7464. A rocking piano bar, long on fun and short on pretense. Expect a lot of audience participation and a songbook heavily weighted with '50s rock, Billy Joel and Elton John standards. No cover before 8 p.m.

JJ's Blues Downtown, 14 S. Second St., San Jose. Tel: 408/286-3066. Next to Toons, this elegantly appointed two-level hall is the place for the blues, from national legends to local wannabes.

Shoreline Amphitheater, 1 Amphitheater Parkway, Mountain View. Tel: 415/967-3000. Big fun under the big top, with a steady diet of national touring rock and pop stars. It's worth paying more for seats in the forward section; the less expensive lawn seating is far less comfortable and far, far, far from the stage. Bring binoculars.

San Jose Live!, in Pavilion Shops, 150 South First St., San Jose. Tel: 408/291-2222. A sprawling, three-clubs-in-one complex featuring a memorabilia-packed sports bar, a disco and a piano bar. A good place to lose yourself in the crowd.

Villa Montalvo, 15400 Montalvo Rd., Saratoga, tel: 408/741-3421, is a center for the arts offering an outdoor professional concert season similar to those of the Mountain Winery and Shoreline Amphitheater, but on a more intimate scale. Classical music, dramatic performances, dance and shows for children also are included.

A sampling of other valley entertainment venues, by category:

Comedy

ComedySportz, 3428 El Camino Real, Santa Clara. Tel: 408/725-1356. Combines improvisational comedy with sport as teams of comics vie to see who wins the best audience reaction, Saturday and Sunday nights only.

Rooster T. Feathers, 157 West El Camino Real, Sunnyvale. Tel: 408/736-0921. A major stop for Bay Area, national comics in a site with historical Silicon Valley significance: the place where the first video game was introduced.

Country & Western

Ozzie Pepper's, South Second St. at Paseo de San Antonio, San Jose. Tel: 408/297-0300. Centrally located in downtown San Jose's Pavilion Shops shopping center, it's a place for urban cowboys and cowgirls to dance and dine.

Horseshoe Club, 2655 El Camino Real, Santa Clara. Tel: 408/248-4100. Basic down home music, dancing.

Dance

D.B. Cooper's, 163 West Santa Clara St., San Jose. Tel: 408/279-5867. D.J. dancing for the younger set. $5 cover.

Oasis, 200 North First St., San Jose. Tel: 408/292-2212. Rock in its various permutations, most often with disc jockeys but some live bands.

Phantom, 5353 Almaden Expressway at Blossom Hill Road, San Jose. Tel: 408/448-7888. Modern rock, D.J. style, big floor.

Sh-Boom, 975 Saratoga-Sunnyvale Rd., San Jose. Tel: 408/725-1600. Emphasis on fifties and sixties classics.

Starlite Ballroom, 2260 North Fair Oaks Ave., Sunnyvale. Tel: 408/745-7827. Shall we waltz? Tango? Foxtrot?

Studio 47, 47 Notre Dame Ave., San Jose. Tel: 408/279-3387. Popular with fans of salsa and other Hispanic rhythms. Large dance floor, often live music. Open to 17 years old and up. Cover from $4–$8.

Jazz/Blues

Club Jazz, 55 South Market St., San Jose. Tel: 408/288-4801. Elegant urban setting, often featuring nationally known jazz headliners. Menu items available from adjoining Gerard's Restaurant. Small cover.

Crazy Horse, 14555 Big Basin Way, Saratoga. Tel: 408/867-4711. Mountain lodge ambiance for intimate jazz evenings. Appetizers and desserts available from adjoining Plumed Horse restaurant. No cover.

Gordon Biersch, 33 East San Fernando St., San Jose. Tel: 408/294-6785. Brewery/restaurant features jazz acts on brick-walled outdoor patio with a distinctly European feel. Big bands perform regularly on warm-weather Sundays.

JJ's Blues Lounge, 3439 Stevens Creek Blvd., San Jose. Tel: 408/243-6441. Strip commercial hole-in-the-wall for the blues basics. Cover Sat. and Sun. only.

JJ's Blues Cafe, 165 East El Camino Real, Mountain View. Tel: 415/968-2277. Somewhat larger version of the preceding, but with the same honest blues. Small cover for some acts.

Number One Broadway, 102B South Santa Cruz Ave., Los Gatos. Tel: 408/354-4303. Varied jazz, jazz-fusion, and blues in suburban second-story setting.

Rock/Pop

Boswell's, in the PruneYard, 1875 South Bascom Ave. and Campbell Avenues, Campbell. Tel: 408/371-4404. Shopping center setting, but a pleasant room featuring local talent.

The Cabaret, 370 Saratoga Ave., San Jose. Tel: 408/248-0641. Good local acts, plus occasional national touring performers.

The Edge, 260 California St., Palo Alto. Tel: 415/324-3343. Another site for local talent, with occasional national acts.

Hard Disk Saloon, 1214 Apollo Way, Sunnyvale. Tel: 408/733-2001. Basic home-grown rock 'n' roll.

Lord John's Inn, 3190 The Alameda, Santa Clara. Tel: 408/984-0475. Pop, occasionally folk and jazz, for the college set near Santa Clara University.

Marsugi's, 399 South First St., San Jose. Tel: 408/286-8345. Downtown basic local rock 'n' roll.

McNeil's, 800 Kiely Blvd., Santa Clara. Tel: 408/244-4038. Local rock, pop acts in a neighborhood setting.

Mountain Charley's, 15 North Santa Cruz Ave., Los Gatos. Tel: 408/395-8880. Former lodge hall-turned-rock emporium for the funkily chic. Small cover.

One Step Beyond, 1400 Martin Ave., Santa Clara. Tel: 408/982-0555. Room to dance for the young and disaffected.

Tied House, 65 North San Pedro St., San Jose. Tel: 408/295-2739. Brewery/restaurant leans toward pop, with occasional jazz.

13
Lodging

Silicon Valley has an ample supply of hotel and motel accommodations, plus a few bed-and-breakfast inns. Prices generally are considered average for the San Francisco Bay Area—lower than those in San Francisco, higher than those in the less populous suburban areas.

Geographically, most hotels and motels are clustered in San Jose, the hub of most transportation facilities; the central region from Milpitas on the east to Cupertino on the west, which offers convenience to both San Jose and the north valley; and the north region, mainly in and around Palo Alto.

Room rates listed below are for two persons per weekday stay, with the lowest for a double room and the highest for a suite. Since most hotel traffic here is of a business nature, not tourist, rates can be substantially lower on weekends and holidays. It also pays to inquire about corporate rates and other reductions offered to members of associations, conventioneers and the like.

Here are the major hostelries, listed by area and by size, with the largest first:

San Jose

Fairmont Hotel, 170 South Market St. Tel: 408/998-1900. 541 rooms. Luxury hotel in the center of the city, within walking distance of San Jose McEnery Convention Center, with two restaurants, fountain/cafe, cabana cafe, lobby lounge, health club, pool. Rates: $155 to $1,800.

Red Lion Hotel, 2050 Gateway Place. Tel: 408/453-4000; 800/547-8010. 507 rooms. Near San Jose International Airport, with restaurant, coffee shop, nightclub, lobby lounge, health club, pool. Rates: $145 to $600.

Hyatt San Jose, 1740 North First St. Tel: 408/993-1234. 474 rooms. Garden-style hotel near San Jose International Airport, with restaurant, bar, coffee shop, pool. Rates: $124 to $650.

San Jose Hilton and Towers, San Carlos Street and Almaden Boulevard, San Jose. Tel: 408/287-2100. 355 rooms. Convention hotel, with pool, restaurant and bar, and featuring indoor access to adjacent San Jose McEnery Convention Center. Rates: $140 to $600.

Le Baron Hotel, 1350 North First St. Tel: 408/453-6200. 327 rooms. The city's most international hotel, on light-rail line between airport and downtown, with restaurant, coffee shop, lobby lounge, pool. Rates: $88 to $700.

Holiday Inn Park Center Plaza, 282 Almaden Blvd. Tel: 408/998-0400. 231 rooms. Across San Carlos Street from convention center, with restaurant, coffee shop/lounge, pool, health club. Rates: $90 to $300.

Motel 6, 2560 Fontaine Rd. Tel: 408/270-3131. 202 rooms. The most basic of basic accommodations, in south San Jose off Highway 101 at the Tully Road exit. Pool. Rate: $36.95; no suites. Also at 2081 North First St., tel 408/436-8180.

Airport Holiday Inn, 1355 North Fourth St. Tel: 408/453-5340. 194 rooms. Located between airport and downtown, near light-rail line, with restaurant, bar and pool. Rate: $83; no suites.

Radisson Plaza Hotel, 1471 North Fourth St. Tel: 408/452-0200; 800/333-3333. 187 rooms. Located between airport and downtown, near light-rail line, with restaurant, bar, health club, pool. Rates: $115 to $375.

Sainte Claire Hotel, Market and San Carlos Streets. Tel: 408/295-2000. 170 rooms. Completely refurbished 1920s hotel, once the city's largest. Located across Market Street from the San Jose McEnery Convention Center, with restaurant, lounge. Rates: $95 to $750.

Courtyard by Marriott, 1727 Technology Dr. Tel: 408/441-6111. 150 rooms. Near airport, with restaurant, lounge. Rates: $99 to $115.

Holiday Inn Silicon Valley, 399 Silicon Valley Blvd. Tel: 408/972-7800. 150 rooms. In south San Jose, off Highway 101 at Bernal Road exit, with restaurant, pool, health club. Rates: $108 to $119.

De Anza Hotel, 233 West Santa Clara St. Tel: 408/286-1000. 101 rooms. Completely refurbished Art Deco landmark in downtown, with restaurant, lounge. Rates: $130 to $750.

Central Silicon Valley

Santa Clara Marriott Hotel, 2700 Mission College Blvd., Santa Clara. Tel: 408/988-1500. 756 rooms. The valley's largest hotel. Located within walking distance of the Great America theme park, with restaurant, coffee shop, lounge, indoor/outdoor pool. Rates: $139 to $400.

Westin Santa Clara Hotel, 5101 Great America Parkway, Santa Clara. Tel: 408/986-0700; 800/228-3000. 500 rooms. Convention hotel, with restaurant, coffee shop, bar, lobby lounge and featuring direct access to the adjacent Santa Clara Convention Center. Rates: $69 to $545.

Sunnyvale Hilton, 1250 Lakeside Dr., Sunnyvale. Tel: 408/738-4888. 372 rooms. Convenient access to Highway 101, with restaurant, lounge, pool. Rates: $120 to $250.

Holiday Inn Milpitas, 777 Bellew Dr., Milpitas. Tel: 408/321-9500. 305 rooms. Restaurant, lounge, fitness facilities, with easy access to I-880 freeway and cross-valley State Route

237. Rates: $102 to $150.

Crown Sterling Suites, 901 East Calaveras Blvd., Milpitas. Tel: 408/942-0400. 267 suites. Features courtyard restaurant and lounge, easy access to I-680 and State Route 237. Rate: $135, includes full breakfast.

Biltmore Hotel, 2151 Laurelwood Rd., Santa Clara. Tel: 408/988-8411. 262 rooms. Near Highway 101 freeway, with restaurant, lounge, lobby bar, pool, exercise facilities. Rates: $144 to $219, includes full breakfast and cocktails.

Residence Inn by Marriott, 750 Lakeway Dr., Sunnyvale. Tel: 408/720-1000; 800/331-3131. 231 rooms. Pool, spas, sports court. Rates: $124 to $149, includes continental breakfast, social hour with beer, wine, hors d'oeuvres.

Sheraton San Jose, 1801 Barber Lane, Milpitas. Tel: 408/943-0600; 800/325-3535. 229 rooms. Near I-880 freeway with restaurant, lounge, pool, fitness room. Rates: $115 to $250.

Quality Suites, 3100 Lakeside Dr., Santa Clara. Tel: 408/748-9800; 800/221-2222. 222 suites. Pool, lounge. Rates: $134 to $154.

Ambassador Business Inn, 910 East Fremont Ave., Sunnyvale. Tel: 408/738-0500. 209 rooms. Pool, health facilities. Rates: $80 to $125.

Beverly Heritage Hotel, 1820 Barber Lane, Milpitas. Tel: 408/943-9080; 800-443-4455. 197 rooms. Near I-880 freeway, with restaurant, lounge, pool, exercise room. Rates: $120 to $165.

Wyndham Garden, 1300 Chesapeake Terrace, Sunnyvale. Tel: 408/747-0999. 180 rooms. Restaurant, lounge, pool, exercise room. Rates: $140 to $160.

Cupertino Inn, 10889 N. De Anza Blvd., Cupertino. Tel: 408/996-7700. 125 rooms. Nearest hotel to Apple Computer, with pool and exercise room. Rates: $119 to $150, includes full breakfast, cocktails.

Palo Alto

Holiday Inn Palo Alto/Stanford, 625 El Camino Real. Tel: 415/328-2800. 355 rooms. Near Stanford University with restaurant, lounge, pool, exercise room. Rates: $134 to $225.

Hyatt Rickey's, 4219 El Camino Real. Tel: 415/493-8000. 347 rooms. Landmark garden-style hotel with restaurant, lounge, pool, croquet, putting green. Rates: $155 to $305.

Hyatt Palo Alto, 4290 El Camino Real. Tel: 415/493-0800. 200 rooms. Restaurant, lounge, tennis court, pool, exercise facilities. Rates: $155 to $210.

Stanford Park Hotel, 100 El Camino Real, Menlo Park. Tel: 415/322-1234. 162 rooms. Northernmost Silicon Valley hotel on Palo Alto/Menlo Park border, with restaurant, lounge, pool, exercise room. Rates: $175 to $265.

Garden Court Hotel, 520 Cowper St. Tel: 415/322-9000. 61 rooms. Downtown Palo Alto location, restaurant. Rates: $170 to $400.

Bed and Breakfast

Briar Rose, 897 E. Jackson St., San Jose. Tel: 408/279-5999. 6 rooms, 4 with bath. Rates: $65 to $125.

Hensley House, 456 N. Third St., San Jose. Tel: 408/298-3537. 5 rooms, each with bath. Rates: $75 to $125.

Madison Street Inn, 1390 Madison St., Santa Clara. Tel: 408/249-5541. 5 rooms, 3 with bath. Rates: $60 to $85.

14
For the Kids

There is no shortage of things to do or places to play for youngsters in Silicon Valley. The valley's benign California climate makes outdoor activities possible throughout much of the year, and for those times when inclement weather takes over, there also are plenty of indoor opportunities.

Nationally known educator Yvette del Prado, formerly superintendent of the Cupertino Union School District and now vice president of education and public affairs for Tandem Computers, recommends these top ten choices:

The Tech Museum of Innovation, 145 West San Carlos St., San Jose. Tel: 408/279-7150. Temporary home of a museum designed to introduce young people ages 10–18 to science and technology as both stimulating entertainment and possible career choices (but adults also can enjoy the exhibits). Included are hands-on exercises in such fields as biotechnology, computer-aided design, robotics, materials science and space exploration. A greatly expanded version of The Tech is planned for Guadalupe River Park in the mid-1990s. Open Tuesday–Sunday, 10 a.m.–5 p.m.

Children's Discovery Museum, 180 Woz Way, Guadalupe River Park, San Jose. Tel: 408/298-5437. Called "the museum with no no-no's," it is a hands-on facility that introduces children 3–13 to the world around them through play. They can descend through a mock utility hole to see what goes on under a city street, clamber over fire engines, design original artwork or learn how water gets from well to faucet, among other things. In Guadalupe River Park, and designed as a complementary twin to The Tech Museum listed above. Open Tues.-Sat., 10–5; Sun. 12–5.

Kelley Park, 1300 Senter Rd., San Jose. Tel: 408/292-8188. This park on the fringe of the center city offers a variety of activities, including an innovative play area known as Happy Hollow, a small zoo, a Japanese garden with pools of colorful koi fish and, immediately adjacent, the San Jose Historical Museum's re-creation of a portion of San Jose's cityscape at the start of the Twentieth Century.

Egyptian Museum and Planetarium, Park and Naglee Avenues, San Jose. Tel: 408/287-2807. The largest collection of Egyptian artifacts, mummies, jewelry and sculpture on the West Coast, including a walk-through replica of an ancient burial tomb. A planetarium and a science center are part of the complex, which also houses the world headquarters of the Rosicrucian Order, an international educational organization. Open daily, 10–5.

Minolta Planetarium, De Anza College, 21250 Stevens Creek Boulevard and Stelling Road, Cupertino. Tel: 408/864-5678. A small but modern planetarium, offering a variety of programs on astronomy and the heavens, on the grounds of the valley's largest community college.

Center for the Performing Arts, Almaden Boulevard at Park Avenue, San Jose. Tel: 408/288-7474. Many performances suitable for children — musical, theatrical, dance — are held regularly throughout the year at this, the valley's largest (2,700 seats) municipal theater facility. The same applies for similarly sized **Flint Center,** De Anza College, Stevens Creek Boulevard and Stelling Road, Cupertino, the valley's largest college theater. Tel: 408/864-8816.

Hakone Gardens, 2100 Big Basin Way, Saratoga. Tel: 408/

741-4994. Created in 1917 and designed by a member of the gardening staff of the emperor of Japan, the gardens offer prime examples of Japanese horticulture and a serene location for spending some quiet time.

The Missions, a replica of the Mission Santa Clara de Asis on the grounds of Santa Clara University, 500 El Camino Real, Santa Clara, and a reconstruction of the Mission San Jose, 43300 Mission Blvd., Fremont, make Father Serra's colonization of Alta California come alive.

The Best of the Rest

Ardenwood Historical Farm, 34600 Ardenwood Blvd., Fremont. Tel: 510/796-0663. Pick crops, cook on a wood-burning stove, bale hay, ride in the horse-drawn wagons.

Barbie Doll Hall of Fame, 460 Waverly St., Palo Alto. Tel: 415/326-5841. More than 1,400 Barbies and Kens in plastic perfection.

Central Park, Kiely Blvd. at Homestead Rd., Santa Clara. Tel: 408/243-7727. Lawns for play, barbecue facilities, space for picnics. It also includes the Santa Clara International Swim Center, training site for Olympic-caliber swimmers but open for swimming by the general public, as well.

Great America, Great America Parkway off Highway 101, Santa Clara. Tel: 408/988-1800. A 100-acre amusement park with roller coasters, assorted thrill rides, shows and concerts.

Northside Theatre Company, tel: 408/288-7820, regularly offers theatrical productions for young people by young people at Olinder Theater, 848 E. William St. at South 18th St., San Jose.

Oak Meadow Park, Blossom Hill Road at University Avenue, Los Gatos. Tel: 408/354-8700. Boasts both a restored carousel and a live-steam railroad connecting with adjoining Vasona Lake County Park.

Prusch Farm Park, 647 S. King Rd., San Jose. Tel: 408/ 926-5555. A turn-of-the-century farmhouse, plus a big barn full of farm animals and a fruit orchard, all in the shadow of modern freeway overpasses.

Raging Waters, Tully and White roads, San Jose. Tel: 408/270-8000. Outdoor water amusement park with water slides, pools for swimming, inner-tube rafting, bodysurfing, and wading. Open May to September

Serra Park, 730 The Dalles Ave., Sunnyvale. A 12-acre playground with whimsical play structures, ponds, and a creek for wading, and ample lawns.

Youth Science Institute (YSI), 16260 Alum Rock Ave., San Jose, Tel: 408/258-4322. Natural history exhibits and displays in San Jose's Alum Rock Park. A YSI branch at Vasona County Park (296 Garden Hill Dr., Los Gatos. Tel: 408/356-4945) offers exhibits of water ecology and wildlife. A third YSI branch in Sanborn County Park (16055 Sanborn Rd., Saratoga. Tel: 408/867-6940) has natural science displays, an insect zoo and reptiles.

15
Sightseeing

Unlimber your camera. While Silicon Valley boasts few singularly spectacular natural wonders of the picture postcard type—no Monterey lone cypress, no Golden Gate Bridge (although both are nearby)—there still are sufficient spots of beauty ample enough to satisfy most photographers.

Professional portrait photographer Paul Tumason of Los Gatos, one of the valley's premier camera artists, suggests these locations as his Top 10 for snapshot-shooting sightseers:

Alviso, the district of San Jose where it meets the southern end of San Francisco Bay; mud flats, watery vistas and picturesque seediness.

Aztec Ridge, only a residential street in Los Gatos, but one offering inspiring views of the valley spreading before you to the north.

Coyote Valley, south of San Jose on Monterey Road (if you get to Morgan Hill you've gone too far) for a glimpse of Silicon Valley's agrarian past—but hurry: it's slated for industrial development.

Fairmont Plaza, between the Fairmont Hotel and San Jose Museum of Art on Market Street in downtown San Jose, where the broad pavement invites people-watching and a circle of palm trees provides punctuation.

The Mountain Winery, 14831 Pierce Rd., Saratoga. Tel: 408/ 741-0445. The view of the valley from its deck is inspiring on a clear day, depressing when smog reminds us how far we still have to go in cleaning up California's air.

Quimby Road, heading east from San Jose toward the Grant Ranch Park—another slice-of-the-past with older orchards and rural vistas.

St. Joseph Cathedral, 80 South Market St., San Jose, tel: 408/292-4124, with its copper domes and beautifully restored interior.

Summit Road, which winds through the spine of the Santa Cruz Mountains from Bear Creek Road to Mount Loma Prieta; redwood country, easily accessible.

The Universities: San Jose State, One Washington Square, San Jose, tel: 408/924-1000, for its ivy-covered tower and grassy quadrangle in the middle of urban San Jose; Santa Clara, 500 El Camino Real, Santa Clara, tel: 408/554-4000, not only for its restored mission but also for the beauty of the surrounding gardens; and Stanford, University Ave. at El Camino Real, Palo Alto, tel: 415/723-2300, for its rolling, rural campus and sandstone-arched buildings.

Villa Montalvo, 15400 Montalvo Rd., Saratoga. Tel: 408/541-3421. Try to get there an hour before sunset, when the light is golden on the 19-room Mediterranean-style Villa built by the late Senator James Phelan. Deer often graze on the mansion's massive front lawn. The estate, open to the public as a center for the arts, also boasts an arboretum with nature trails for hiking and a virtually year-round series of concerts, recitals and theatrical events.

The Best of the Rest

Carmelite Monastery, 1000 Lincoln St., Santa Clara, tel: 408/296-8412. Spanish Ecclesiastical architecture on a portion of an original Spanish land grant.

Indian Center of San Jose, 919 The Alameda, San Jose, tel: 408/971-9622. Artifacts, biographers of famous Native

American leaders, dioramas, arts and crafts in a center American Indian-owned and operated.

Japanese Friendship Tea Garden, in Kelley Park, Senter Road and Keyes St., San Jose, tel: 408/287-2290. A copy of the Korakuen Gardens in San Jose's Japanese sister city, Okayama. Lovely cherry blossoms in the spring.

Libby Can Water Tower, Mathilda and California Avenues, Sunnyvale. A reminder of the valley's past as a fruit-producing and canning center, this water tower—still in use—is painted to resemble an early 1900s fruit cocktail can.

Lick Observatory, Highway 130 east of San Jose atop Mt. Hamilton, tel: 408/274-5061. A working astronomical observatory, administered by the University of California, and the burial place of its donor, philanthropist James Lick.

New Almaden, Almaden Road at Bertram Road. The village that once provided residences for workers of the adjacent New Almaden mercury mine; a number of the original buildings still are intact and in use.

Overfelt Gardens Park, 1776 Educational Park Dr., San Jose, tel: 408/251-3323. Included among its lawns, gardens and streams are monuments to Chinese culture: statuary, an impressive gate, an ornate meeting house. There's also a fragrance garden for the visually impaired.

Plaza Park, Market Street between San Fernando and San Carlos Streets, San Jose. Not a spectacular park by most standards, but watch the interaction between passersby, especially children, and the spurting fountains near the Fairmont Hotel—a photographer's delight.

Rosicrucian Egyptian Museum and Art Gallery, Park and Naglee Avenues, San Jose, tel: 408/287-2807. The museum looks like something straight off the Nile; its gardens also provide some scenic photo opportunities.

San Jose Flea Market, 12000 Berryessa Rd., San Jose, tel: 408/453-1110. An average of more than 2,700 sellers on its

120 acres make this open-air flea market among the nation's biggest.

San Jose Historical Museum, Senter Road adjacent to Japanese Friendship Tea Garden, San Jose, tel: 408/287-2290. Re-creates portions of San Jose as it looked at the turn of the century.

San Jose Municipal Rose Garden, Naglee Ave. at Dana Ave., San Jose, tel: 408/287-0698. Six acres with 7,000 plantings of more than 150 varieties of roses. Best time to visit is between mid-May and November.

Santa Clara sculptures: the statue of Our Lady of Peace, 2800 Mission College Blvd., Santa Clara, near Highway 101, a stainless steel work by Charles Parks (also referred to as "Our Lady of the Freeway"); Saint Clare, Lincoln St. at El Camino Real, a bronze by Anne Van Kleeck; and the Universal Child, Lincoln and Warburton Avenues, Santa Clara, a steel and mosaic tile creation by Beniamino Bufano.

Sunset Magazine, Middlefield and Willow Roads, Menlo Park, tel: 415/321-3600. Long the Bible of western gardeners, Sunset Magazine maintains beautifully landscaped grounds demonstrating the best of its horticultural prowess. Free 45-minute tours are offered Monday through Friday at 10:30 a.m. and 2:30 p.m.

Winchester Mystery House, 525 South Winchester Blvd., San Jose, tel: 408/247-2101. The unfinished, 160-room mansion of firearms heiress Sarah Winchester, geared toward tourists but still interesting for its architectural oddities.

16
Sports

This is California, where the weather more often than not permits inhabitants to be out of doors without hardship. As a result, most Californians do more playing themselves than watching others play. Either way, Silicon Valley offers ample opportunities for both.

Participatory Sports

GOLF

Blackberry Farm, 22100 Stevens Creek Blvd., Cupertino. Tel: 408/253-9200. 9 holes, pro shop, putting green, driving range, restaurant. Cost: $7.50 weekdays, $9.25 weekends.

Deep Cliff Golf Course, 10700 Clubhouse Lane, Cupertino. Tel: 408/253-5357. 18 holes, pro shop, restaurant, putting green. Cost: $20 weekdays, $27 weekends ($15/$19 after 2 p.m.; $10/$12 for 9 holes after 2 p.m.).

Gavilan Golf Course, 5055 Santa Teresa Blvd., Gilroy. Tel: 408/848-1363. 9 holes, driving range, putting green, restaurant, barbecue area. Cost: $10 weekdays, $13 weekends.

Hill Country Golf Course, 15060 Foothill Ave., Morgan Hill. Tel: 408/779-4136. 18 holes, pro shop, putting green, restaurant. Cost: $12 weekdays, $15 weekends.

Palo Alto Municipal Golf Course, 1875 Embarcadero Rd., Palo

Alto. Tel: 415/856-0881. 18 holes, pro shop, restaurant, putting green, driving range, practice bunker. Cost: $16 weekdays, $20 weekends ($11/$14 after 3 p.m.).

Pleasant Hills Golf & Country Club, 2050 South White Rd., San Jose. Tel: 408/238-3485. 18 holes, pro shop. Cost: $18 weekdays, $23 weekends.

Pruneridge Golf Club, 400 North Saratoga Ave., Santa Clara. Tel: 408/248-4424. 9 holes, pro shop, driving range, putting green, chipping area, snack bar. Cost: $8 weekdays, $9.50 weekends.

Riverside Golf Club, Monterey Highway at Sycamore Avenue, San Jose. Tel: 408/463-0622. 18 holes, pro shop, driving range, putting green, restaurant. Cost: $20 weekdays, $27 weekends (after 1 p.m., rates vary).

San Jose Municipal Golf Course, 1560 Oakland Rd., San Jose. Tel: 408/441-4653. 18 holes, pro shop, driving range, putting green, restaurant. Cost: $22 weekdays, $30 weekends ($13/$16 after 3 p.m.).

Santa Clara Golf & Tennis Club, 5155 Stars & Stripes Dr., Santa Clara. Tel: 408/980-9515. 18 holes, pro shop, driving range, putting green, restaurant, tennis courts with own pro shop. Cost: $18 weekdays, $24 weekends ($13/$16 after 3 p.m.).

Santa Teresa Golf Club, 260 Bernal Rd., San Jose. Tel: 408/225-2650. 18 holes, pro shop, driving range, putting green, restaurant. Cost: $24 weekdays, $34 weekends ($14/$18 after 3 p.m.).

Shoreline Golf Links, 2600 North Shoreline Blvd., Mountain View. Tel: 415/969-2041. 18 holes, pro shop, driving range, putting green, snack bar. Cost: $29 weekdays, $38 weekends ($22/$31 after 3 p.m.).

Spring Valley Golf Course, 3441 East Calaveras Blvd., Milpitas. Tel: 408/262-1722. 18 holes, pro shop, driving range, putting green, chipping area, restaurant. Cost: $20 weekdays,

$28 weekends ($14/$16 after 2:30 p.m.).

Summit Pointe Golf Club, 1500 Country Club Dr., Milpitas. Tel: 408/262-8813. 18 holes, pro shop, driving range, putting green, restaurant. Cost: $20 weekdays, $32 weekends ($15/$27 after 2 p.m.).

Sunken Gardens Golf Course, 1010 North Wolfe Rd., Sunnyvale. Tel: 408/739-6588. 9 holes, pro shop, driving range, putting green, restaurant. Cost: $7.75 weekdays, $10 weekends.

Sunnyvale Municipal Golf Course, 605 Macara Rd., Sunnyvale. Tel: 408/738-3666. 18 holes, pro shop, restaurant, putting green. Cost: $18 weekdays, $23 weekends ($12/$15 after 3 p.m.).

Thunderbird Golf and Country Club, 221 South King Rd., San Jose. Tel: 408/259-3355. 18 holes, driving range, putting green, snack bar. Cost: $14 weekdays, $17 weekends ($11/$14 after 3 p.m.).

HIKING/JOGGING/CYCLING

Mid-Peninsula Regional Open Space District, 201 San Antonio Circle, Suite C-135, Mountain View. Tel: 415/949-5500. Offers information on more than 200 miles of trails at various Santa Clara County outdoor preserves.

ICE SKATING

Eastridge Ice Arena, Eastridge Mall, Tully Rd. at Capitol Ave., San Jose. Tel: 408/238-0440.

Ice Capades Chalet, Vallco Fashion Park, Wolfe Rd. at I-280, Cupertino. Tel: 408/446-2906.

SAILING

Lake Cunningham Park, 2305 South White Rd., San Jose. Tel: 408/277-4319.

Vasona Park, Blossom Hill Rd. at Highway 17, Los Gatos. Tel: 408/395-6755.

SWIMMING

Campbell Community Center, 1 West Campbell Ave., Campbell. Tel: 408/866-2105.

Rinconada Community Pool, Embarcadero Rd. at Newell Rd., Palo Alto. Tel: 415/329-2261.

Santa Clara International Swim Center, 2625 Patricia Dr., Santa Clara. Tel: 408/243-7727.

TENNIS

Backesto Park, North 13th St. at Mission St., San Jose. Eight lighted courts.

Greer Park, 1098 Amarillo Ave., Palo Alto. Four unlighted courts.

John McEnery Park, West San Fernando St. near Market St., San Jose. Four lighted courts.

Mitchell Park, 600 East Meadow Dr., Palo Alto. Seven lighted courts.

Rinconada Park, 777 Embarcadero Rd., Palo Alto. Six lighted and 3 unlighted courts.

Memorial Park, Mary Ave. and Stevens Creek Blvd., Cupertino. Six lighted courts.

Las Animas Park, Park Dr. and Church St., Gilroy. Three lighted courts.

Pinewood Park, Starlight Drive and Lonetree Court. Four lighted courts.

Community Park, Edmundson Ave. near Monterey, Morgan Hill. Two lighted courts.

Calabazas Park, Blaney Ave. and Rainbow Drive, San Jose. Three courts.

Central Park, 969 Kiely Blvd. near Homestead Rd., San

Jose. Twelve lighted courts.

WINDSURFING

Los Gatos Creek Park, 1200 Dell Ave., Campbell. Tel: 408/356-2729.

Lexington Reservoir, Highway 17 at Alma Bridge Rd., Los Gatos. Tel: 408/356-2729.

Professional Sports

BASEBALL

San Jose Giants, Class A California League. Municipal Stadium, Senter Road and Alma Street, San Jose. Tel: 408/297-1435.

HOCKEY

San Jose Sharks, National Hockey League, tel: 408/287-4275. Team plays on home ice at the San Jose Arena, West Santa Clara St. at Montgomery St., San Jose.

SOCCER

San Francisco Bay Blackhawks, tel: 510/736-6801, play both professional and semi-pro teams from the United States and foreign countries. Games at Spartan Stadium, 10th and Alma streets, San Jose.

Colleges

San Jose State University Spartans play a near-complete schedule of NCAA Division 1-A sports. Tel: 408/924-3267. Football games are played at Spartan Stadium, 10th and Alma Streets; basketball games at the Event Center, Seventh and San Carlos streets; and baseball games at San Jose Municipal

Stadium, Senter Road and Alma Street, all in San Jose.

Santa Clara University Broncos participate in NCAA Division II sports. Tel: 408/554-4660. Baseball games are played at Buck Shaw Stadium, basketball games at Toso Pavilion. Both are on the SCU campus, 500 El Camino Real, Santa Clara.

Stanford University Cardinal plays a full schedule of NCAA Division 1-A sports. Tel: 800/232-8225; 415/723-1021. Football games are played at Stanford Stadium, basketball games at Maples Pavilion and baseball games at Sunken Diamond. All are located on the Stanford campus, El Camino Real at University Avenue, Palo Alto.

17
Shopping

No shopping expedition to Silicon Valley is complete without a visit to Fry's Electronics. The lure isn't so much in the products available, but for the opportunity it offers the visitor to get next to the typical valley tech-types in their own lair, to see what they consider important and, perhaps, to learn why.

Fry's aren't simply electronics stores, you see, although they stock everything electronic from the simplest consumer goods such as clock radios and television sets to the most esoteric of computer equipment and peripherals, sufficient for the knowledgeable to build a mainframe from the ground up. What's different about Fry's is that their stores also stock foodstuffs and variety items on aisles adjoining the assorted widgets, rather like a supermarket with some really exotic equipment.

Indeed, Fry's was founded as a valley supermarket chain by Charles Fry, but three sons—John, Randy and David Fry—took the family into technology in 1985, selling off the markets and opening a Sunnyvale electronics store-with-munchies.

It became an instant success, fueled by shoppers following this scenario: Tech-type constructing own electronics equipment or laboring over computer program discovers he needs a part or technical advice, rushes to Fry's, picks up same, sees food, realizes he has been so engrossed in work he hasn't eaten in ten hours, buys edibles, realizes he'll eventually need razor blades and toilet paper and buys those, too, and then returns to job, only to repeat process the following day, thankful that he can find most of life's basic needs—widgets and food—under one time-saving roof. Silicon Valley's obsessive technological lifestyle, succored and satisfied. If sex could be sold legally at Fry's, it's conceivable the techies wouldn't have to go anywhere else.

Fry's Electronics operates stores in Sunnyvale at 1177 Kern Ave., tel: 408/733-1770; in Palo Alto at 340 Portage Ave., tel: 415/496-6000 and in Fremont at 440 Mission Ct., tel: 510/3797.

Other superstores offering competitive technological products include: **BizMart,** in Santa Clara at 2790 El Camino Real, tel: 408/261-7520; **CompUSA** in Santa Clara at El Camino Real and Lawrence Expressway, tel: 408/554-1733; and **Computer Attic** in Cupertino at 10251 South De Anza Blvd., tel: 408/253-5300. But you'll have to bring your own M&Ms.

When it comes to non-technical shopping—just the basic browsing and buying so beloved in the rest of the United States—the pecking order in Silicon Valley follows roughly the adage that west is best, east costs least and north usually tops south. This is mall country, for the most part, where enclosed shopping centers usually do the greater volume of business and offer the greater variety of stores (with the exception of Stanford Shopping Center, where the mix of haute couture stores and its proximity to monied shoppers overcomes its open-air design). Certain cities or districts also are noted for their distinctive shopping opportunities separate from the chain-store mall operations.

Major Malls

Valley Fair, Stevens Creek Blvd. at Highway 17, San Jose. Nordstrom, Macy's, Emporium. The valley's largest with 175 stores.

Stanford, El Camino Real and Quarry Rd., Palo Alto. Neiman Marcus, Saks Fifth Avenue, Nordstrom, Macy's, Emporium. 140 stores.

Vallco Fashion Park, Wolfe Rd. at I-280, Cupertino. Emporium, J.C. Penney, Sears. 175 stores.

Eastridge Shopping Center, Tully Rd. and Capitol Expy., San Jose. Macy's, Sears, J.C. Penney. 160 stores.

Oakridge Mall, Pearl Ave., Blossom Hill Rd. and Santa Teresa, San Jose. Nordstrom, Macy's, Ward. 110 stores.

Sunnyvale Town Center, Mathilda and Washington Avenues, Sunnyvale. Macy's, Ward. 120 stores.

San Antonio Shopping Center, El Camino Real and San Antonio Rd., Mountain View. Sears, Mervyn's. 120 stores.

Westgate Shopping Center, Campbell and Saratoga Avenues, San Jose. Ward, Home Express, Burlington Coat Factory. 85 stores.

Open Air Centers

Town & Country Village, El Camino Real and Embarcadero Rd., Palo Alto. 90 stores.

Town & Country Village, Stevens Creek and Winchester Boulevards, San Jose. 90 stores.

Almaden Plaza, Almaden Expressway and Blossom Hill Rd., San Jose. 50 stores.

Capitol Square, North Capitol Ave. and McKee Rd., San Jose. 45 stores.

The Oaks, Stevens Creek Blvd. at Highway 85, Cupertino. 38 stores.

Cities

The following suburbs offer interesting mixes of boutiques, antiques and smaller, individualized stores on some of their thoroughfares:

Los Gatos, particularly along Santa Cruz Avenue and Main Street.

Menlo Park, centered along Santa Cruz Avenue west of El Camino Real.

Palo Alto, along University Avenue east from El Camino Real.

Districts

Japantown, in San Jose surrounding the intersection of North Fifth and Jackson streets, provides shopping, galleries, dining and homey pleasures for travelers, expatriates and Japanese-Americans alike.

The **Willow Glen** district of San Jose, along Lincoln Avenue largely between Willow Street and Minnesota Avenue, also offers interesting browsing for the non-mall shopper.

The Bargain Basement

Pacific West Outlet Center, located on Leavesly Road just off Highway 101 in the south Silicon Valley city of Gilroy, is a shopping center made up only of manufacturers' outlet stores and discount or off-price stores. Nike, Gitano, Joan & David, Fila, Esprit, among others. Tel: 408/847-4155.

San Jose Flea Market, 12000 Berryessa Rd., San Jose. Tel: 408-453-1110. Bills itself as the "world's largest flea market and Northern California's largest farmers' market." At 120 acres and 2,700 vendor spaces, that might not be an exaggeration. Open Wednesday through Sunday. Parking fee is $3; no admission charge.

18
Wineries

It doesn't get the acclaim of Napa and Sonoma, its more famous valley neighbors to the north, but the Santa Clara Valley and its surrounding hillsides also are home to a number of wineries—from large producers to small boutique types—that also produce quality California wines. The ones listed below offer daily tastings to the public and many also have tours by appointment for those who care to see how the valley's agricultural past is tastefully continuing into the future.

Byington Winery, 21850 Bear Creek Rd., Los Gatos. Tel: 408/354-1111.

Congress Springs Vineyards, 13600 Congress Springs Rd., Saratoga. Tel: 408/867-1409.

Emilio Guglielmo Winery, 480 East Main Ave., Morgan Hill. Tel: 408/779-2145.

Fortino Winery, 4525 Hecker Pass Highway, Gilroy. Tel: 408/842-3305.

Hecker Pass Winery, 4605 Hecker Pass Highway, Gilroy. Tel: 408/842-8755.

J. Lohr Winery, 1000 Lenzen Ave. at The Alameda, San Jose. Tel: 408/288-5057.

Kirigin Cellars, 11550 Watsonville Rd., Gilroy. Tel: 408/847-8827.

Mirassou Champagne Cellars, 300 College Ave., Los Gatos. Tel: 408/395-3790.

Mirassou Vineyards, 3000 Aborn Rd., San Jose. Tel: 408/274-4000.

Pedrizzetti Winery, 1645 San Pedro Ave., Morgan Hill. Tel: 408/779-7389.

Rapazzini Winery, Hwy 101 and Hwy 25, Gilroy. Tel: 408/842-5849.

Thomas Kruse Winery, 4390 Hecker Pass Highway, Gilroy. Tel: 408/842-7016.

Other, smaller wineries also offer tastings, although not on a daily basis, and some also offer tours by appointment. For information about specific wineries and/or labels, the Santa Clara Valley Wine Growers Association offers assistance. Its mailing address is P.O. Box 1192, Morgan Hill, CA 95037. Tel: 408/842-5649 or 408/778-1555.

19
The Great Outdoors

Silicon Valley's greatest natural asset, besides the brains of its inhabitants, is its weather. The basically benign climate encourages residents and visitors alike to spend as much time out of doors as possible. Here are some areas of open space where nature is preserved and human participation welcomed.

Almaden Quicksilver County Park, 21785 Almaden Rd., San Jose. Tel: 408/268-8220. Located at the end of Almaden road in south San Jose, the park offers visitors a look at the former operations of the historic New Almaden mercury mines (although the mines themselves are off-limits for safety reasons). An easy hike up Mine Hill Trail begins at the park headquarters.

Alum Rock Park, end of Alum Rock Avenue, San Jose. Tel: 408/259-5477. A city-maintained, 700-acre park for hiking, horseback riding, bicycling and picnicking. Sample the mineral water bubbling from springs there if you dare (or if you're particularly fond of sulphur); at the turn of the century, the water was considered to have healthful properties.

Anderson Lake County Park, 59 Burnett Avenue, Morgan Hill. Tel: 408/779-3634. This 6,301-acre county park offers a variety of water sports, hiking trails and picnic areas. Power boating and water skiing are popular pastimes on the lake itself, actually Santa Clara County's largest reservoir.

Baylands Park, Embarcadero Road east from Highway 101, Palo Alto. Tel: 415/329-2506. Catwalks extending over marshy baylands offer a chance for close-up viewing of the flora and fauna that flourish along the edges of San Francisco Bay. It's particularly picturesque at sunrise and sunset, and, because of the usual northwesterly winds in the afternoons, an almost foolproof place to get kites easily airborne.

Calero Lake County Park, 23201 McKean Road, San Jose. Tel: 268-3883. A 2,284-acre park surrounding a man-made reservoir, it features sandy beaches and picnic areas, plus water-skiing and jet-skiing on the lake. Stables also are available for horse rentals.

Coyote Lake County Park, 10840 Coyote Lake Road, Gilroy. Tel: 408/842-7800. Similar to the aforementioned Calero Lake, Coyote is a 760-acre park for picnicking, camping, fishing, hiking and boating.

Henry W. Coe State Park, end of Dunne Avenue, 14 miles east of Morgan Hill. Tel: 408/779-2728. The largest state park in Northern California at 68,000 acres, this mammoth preserve of largely wild land offers backpacking and primitive camping opportunities galore. Trails and dirt roads are open to hikers, mountain bikers and horseback riders. If getting away from it all is your desire, Coe is the place. Its spring wildflowers are particularly spectacular.

Grant Ranch Park, Mount Hamilton Road, San Jose. Tel: 408/274-6121. Located east of San Jose on the twisting road to Mount Hamilton and Lick Observatory, this former cattle ranch gives visitors a taste of what life was like in California's rural past. Horses are available for rental. Fishing and hiking also are popular pastimes.

Guadalupe Oak Grove, McAbee and Thorntree streets, San Jose. Tel: 408/277-4661. This city park offers 60 acres of mature oak trees, picnic areas, hiking trails with wheelchair access, and hilltop views.

Jasper Ridge Biological Preserve, adjacent to Stanford University. Open October through June, the preserve's most spectacular feature is its spring wildflowers. Docent-led tours of this 1,200-acre outdoor university laboratory may be arranged by calling 415/327-2277.

Lake Cunningham, South White and Tully roads, San Jose. Tel: 408/277-4319. Although this city park is surrounded by metropolis, it nevertheless offers 200 acres of open space including its namesake lake for fishing and boating (no motor boats, rentals available). There also are playgrounds, paths for hiking and bicycle riding, picnic areas, barbecues, a large lawn area for games and the Raging Waters water-slide theme park.

Ed R. Levin Park, 3100 East Calaveras Rd., Milpitas. Tel: 408/262-6980. Tucked into the eastern foothills above Milpitas, this park offers boating, fishing, hiking, horseback riding and windsurfing.

Lexington Reservoir County Park, Highway 17 at Alma Bridge Road, Los Gatos. Tel: 408/867-0190. Sailboating and fishing are the features of this 844-acre park surrounding a man-made reservoir. Power boating is not permitted.

Mid-Peninsula Open Space District, 201 San Antonio Circle, Suite C-135, Mountain View. Tel: 415/949-5500. It maintains more than 200 miles of hiking trails, concentrated in the western foothills from San Carlos to Los Gatos. There also are docent-led walks. Call or write for a free guide.

Prusch Farm Park, South King and Story roads, San Jose. Tel: 408/926-5555. Another open area surrounded by the city, this 47-acre enclave preserves a look at San Jose's rural past. There's a large lawn, historic farm house, barn, livestock and community gardens.

Rancho San Antonio, Cristo Rey Drive, Mountain View. Tel: 408/867-3654. This county park offers hiking trails through rolling, oak-dotted hills for the adventuresome, plus other trails gentle enough for families pushing strollers. Families also can enjoy Deer Hollow Farm, a working farm on the property with typical farm animals present for up-close viewing.

Sanborn-Skyline County Park, 16055 Sanborn Rd., Saratoga. Tel: 408/867-9959. Five miles into the Santa Cruz Mountains above Saratoga, this park offers camping, hiking and horseback riding in the redwoods.

Uvas Canyon County Park, Croy Road, Morgan Hill. Tel: 408/779-9232. A 1,077-acre park offering picnicking, camping and hiking in a particularly pleasant canyon. In spring, the cascading waterfall on Swanson Creek is a popular attraction.

20
Annual Events

Festivals, fiestas, fairs and other annual events pop up almost every month in and around Silicon Valley. With a few exceptions, such as Fourth of July events, most will vary from date to date each year depending on the individual year's calendar. Precise dates, times and admission fees, if any, are available by calling the Visitor Information Center, 408/283-8833, or from the recorded FYI Line, 408/295-2265. The San Jose Convention and Visitors Bureau also provides information, 408/295-9600.

The year's major events:

January

East-West Shrine Football Classic. A college all-star football game, featuring top graduating seniors organized into two teams representing the eastern and western halves of the United States and coached by leading collegiate coaches. It also offers a lavish half-time spectacle — and a good opportunity for pro football scouts to check out the year's talent in the collegiate football draft. Sponsored by the region's Shrine clubs, the game benefits the Shriners' Hospitals for disabled and burned children and is played at Stanford Stadium.

February–March

Tet Festival. This is the Southeast Asian New Year's

celebration, an occasion for great celebration particularly among Santa Clara Valley's Vietnamese population, which is the largest in Northern California. They mark the event with dancing and food, arts and crafts and cultural exhibits. Open to the public at large, at Santa Clara County Fairgrounds.

Chinese New Year's. New Year's, as calculated on the Chinese lunar calendar, also is an occasion for celebration. Its most visible public manifestation in Silicon Valley is in Mountain View, where a full-scale parade with traditional lion dancers and the multi-segmented dragon wind their way along Castro Street through the center of downtown. Since Castro Street also offers the region's largest concentration of Asian restaurants, traditional New Year's feasting also is a popular attraction.

April

Nikkei Matsuri Festival. It's spring, the fruit trees are bursting with blooms and Japan traditionally celebrates. The same applies with Japanese-Americans in Silicon Valley, who mark the occasion with traditional costumed dancers and a variety of food and cultural booths in San Jose's Japantown, centered around N. Fifth and Jackson streets.

May

Cinco de Mayo. Silicon Valley's Mexican-American population, the largest in Northern California, celebrates the May 5 victory during Mexico's war for independence with a colorful parade winding through downtown San Jose, principally along West Santa Clara and Market streets. Afterwards, the crowd enjoys day-long musical and cultural entertainment and exhibits, plus food and refreshment booths located in the Plaza Park area.

Mushroom Mardi Gras. Fungus is seldom celebrated, but

Morgan Hill is a major mushroom-producing area and annually celebrates its major crop each Memorial Day. How do you like your mushrooms? Sauteed? Marinated? Raw? As a subject for art or crafts? It's all here, and more, at Morgan Hill Community Park. The event benefits local schools and non-profit organizations.

June

Living History Days. Costumed docents re-create life in turn-of-the-century Santa Clara Valley at the San Jose Historical Museum, 1600 Senter Rd., San Jose, a 25-acre outdoor museum with original and replica buildings from the city's past. Quilters quilt, weavers weave, blacksmiths work their forges and an antique trolley even rattles through town.

Juneteenth. This is a celebration of African-American history and culture, modeled after similar celebrations following emancipation. Dances, songs and cultural exhibits from the United States, Africa, the Caribbean, and Central and South America are featured, along with a variety of food and refreshments. The festival has been held in recent years at the south campus area of San Jose State University, South 10th and Alma Streets.

July

Gilroy Garlic Festival. If you thought mushrooms were an unusual crop to celebrate, make way for garlic. Gilroy's annual festival offers everything you wanted to know or taste or smell about garlic, from gourmet fare to garlic ice cream. Food booths abound, there are arts and crafts exhibits and a variety of stage entertainment during the two-day weekend fete, held at Gilroy's Christmas Hill Park. The event benefits local schools and non-profit organizations. Breath mints are a must.

San Jose America Festival. This is a mammoth, multi-day

festival celebrating America's and San Jose's cultural diversity, usually centered around Independence Day. Concerts, dramatic presentations, an international mariachi festival, a wide variety of folkloric dance performances, art exhibits from classical to avant garde and a spectacular Fourth of July fireworks display are some of the major attractions. Most events are held in and around downtown San Jose. In 1992, the fireworks alone attracted a crowd estimated at 80,000.

August

San Jose Jazz Festival. A weekend festival of America's own music, with international, national and local jazz performers holding forth on five or more outdoor stages throughout downtown San Jose. Also included are art exhibits and a variety of food and refreshment booths, plus indoor club performances and cinematic offerings. Most of the performances are free. Approximately 60,000 persons attended the festival in 1992.

Santa Clara County Fair. Northern California's largest county fair, with more than 170 acres of exhibits, attractions and carnival rides. While it harkens back to the valley's rural past with exhibits of fruit, livestock and handicrafts, it also makes a bow to today with exhibits of modern technology and modern entertainers. The fair normally runs slightly more than two weeks at the Santa Clara County Fairgrounds, 344 Tully Rd., San Jose.

September

Tapestry in Talent. This is the valley's largest arts and crafts festival, spreading from Plaza Park westward along Park Avenue in downtown San Jose over the Labor Day weekend. Subtitled "The Great American Arts Festival," it includes arts and crafts demonstrations, materials for sale, continuous live entertainment and a wide variety of food and refreshment booths.

Mexican Independence Day. The valley's large Mexican-American community celebrates Mexico's independence from Spain, usually on the weekend closest to September 16, with a parade and booths offering traditional foods, crafts and entertainment in downtown San Jose.

October

Italian-American Cultural Festival. Italian-Americans re-create an Italian village at the Santa Clara County Fairgrounds, filling it with decorated booths, painted carts and dancers doing the tarantella. There are food booths, chances to play bocce ball, and entertainment from grand opera to pop.

November

Veterans Day Parade. Silicon Valley marks Veterans Day each November 11 with a multi-division parade of military and civilian bands, mounted units, drill teams and military vehicles and ordnance, usually led by a high-ranking grand marshal and often featuring fly-bys of military aircraft and sky-diving exhibitions. It's a full-scale, flag-waving salute to the nation's service men and women.

December

Christmas in the Park. Years ago, mortician Don Lima attracted crowds to his funeral parlor with an outdoor display of animated elves and other Christmas figures. When the display—and the traffic—grew too great, he donated the figures to the City of San Jose, where parks department employees and a large cadre of volunteers have continued to expand and upgrade the show into a seasonal display of animated exhibits for children, filling downtown San Jose's

Plaza Park and stretching eastward along the Paseo de San Antonio. A night-time parade, with Santa Claus arriving aboard a fire truck, opens the Christmas in the Park display, usually a week or two before Christmas, and the exhibits remain on display through New Year's. The snow may not be real, but the look of enchantment in children's eyes certainly is. There is no charge to view the display.

21
Handling the Holidays

Should you be lucky enough to visit Silicon Valley during holiday seasons, you'll be able to experience the special ambience the valley gives to these observances. Here are some suggestions to make your holiday time in Silicon Valley more special:

Christmas/New Year's

Start one of your days with breakfast at the San Jose Fairmont Hotel's Fountain restaurant (170 South Market St.,) a '90s soda fountain with a special flair for breakfast fare. Being there also gives you a chance to check out the hotel's lavish lobby display — six-foot tall chocolate nutcrackers, a chocolate toy train running through a chocolate forest. It's chocoholics' heaven.

Stroll across Market Street to view the Christmas in the Park displays. Entirely covering Plaza Park, the lighted Christmas trees and animated Yuletide displays are an annual delight, especially to families with small children. Being a kid makes it easier to forget that the "snow" actually is cotton batting, a concession to the mild California climate. But return to the display at night, when darkness helps hide the snow's cotton seams and twinkling lights work their magic, and even kids in their fifties and beyond can become transfixed.

Get into the spirit of Christmas Past by visiting the San

Jose Historical Museum, a short drive east of downtown at the corner of Alma and Senter Roads. Its reconstruction of turn-of-the-century San Jose, with docents in period costumes at many of the Victorian homes, will transport you to another era.

The lovely carpenter-Gothic Trinity Episcopal Cathedral at 81 North Second St., overlooking downtown San Jose's St. James Park, also evokes images of the valley's earlier days and provides a welcome respite from the holiday's more secular aspects.

Then let yourself be entertained by "The Nutcracker" ballet (it's produced annually by a number of ballet companies, from the professional San Jose Cleveland Ballet to smaller but no less sincere amateur companies; call the Convention & Visitors Bureau's hot line, 408/283-8833, for times and locations) or take in one of the holiday theatrical performances by the San Jose Repertory Theater (408/291-2255) or Palo Alto's TheaterWorks (415/323-8311).

For New Year's revelry, all of the valley's major hotels (and some of its smaller ones, too) offer room/dinner/party packages. And recover New Year's Day by watching the bowl games with the other sports fanatics at San Jose Live! at the Pavilion, 150 South First St.

Valentine's Day

Romance is in the air, and the California hills surrounding Silicon Valley are beginning to look their best, carpeted in velvety new grasses. It's the perfect time for a drive — in a convertible with the top down, if the weather is cooperative — to the Stanford Art Gallery's Rodin Garden. It offers a truly impressive collection of bronzes by the master French sculptor — the human body in its myriad of forms, on view as you stroll arm-in-arm along the garden's paths. The Rodin riches are easy to find: just look for the landmark Hoover

Tower on the Stanford University campus; the gallery is near-by on Serra street.

While you're in the area, consider stopping for lunch at Chez Louis, 4170 El Camino Real, in Palo Alto. Long a hangout for Stanford undergrads and alumni when it was known as L'Omelette, Chez Louis today offers romantic French fare prepared by Chef Louis Borel. But don't stuff yourself; there's more to come later.

If the weather isn't cooperative or if driving is inconvenient, San Jose Museum of Art at 110 South Market St. occasionally offers an impressive collection of smaller Rodin bronzes in its upstairs gallery. Why so much stress on Rodin for Valentine's? If you think of his statue, "The Kiss," you'll know.

For the perfect Valentine's dinner (this is why you took it easy at Chez Louis), try to get a place at the annual Mirassou Winery Valentine's extravaganza meals. They feature a sensuous menu of legendary aphrodisiac fare (real aphrodisiacs? imagined? the mind is the key here), and accompanied, of course, by specially selected wines. The meals usually are served on two nights: one at Mirassou's San Jose's winery, 3000 Aborn Rd., and the other at its Los Gatos champagne cellars, 300 College Ave. Reservations are required, and may lovers' luck be with you when you call 408/274-4000.

Easter

Eggs for breakfast, of course, and there's no place in Silicon Valley that makes such a big deal of breakfast as the small suburb of Los Gatos. Many of the restaurants along Santa Cruz Avenue or Main Street specialize in breakfast, and most are well worth the wait that's often necessary to get in. Some of the best: Breakfast Club, 337 North Santa Cruz Ave.; The Diner of Los Gatos, 235 Saratoga Ave.; Great Bear Coffee & Los Osos Cafe, 19 North Santa Cruz Ave.;

Los Gatos Cafe, 340 North Santa Cruz Ave.; and the Southern Kitchen, 27 East Main St.

Respect the religious nature of Easter with visits to either St. Joseph Cathedral in downtown San Jose (80 South Market St.) or Stanford Memorial Church (on the Stanford University campus in Palo Alto). The former is a wonderfully restored 1880s edifice with architecture based on the classic cross concept; the latter is a prime example of Stanford's red-tile, California sandstone architecture, and both can buoy the soul—no matter what your religion or belief—just by walking through their doors. If Stanford is your choice, then note that springtime in California means flowers aplenty, and few places show off flowers to better advantage than the nearby Filoli Mansion on Canada Rd., south of Highway 92 in Woodside (415/364-2880). The 42-room mansion, used as the setting for TV's "Dynasty," is one of the few country homes in California that has its grounds, all 654 acres of them, still intact, and many are planted with lovely formal gardens, open to the public.

If St. Joseph Cathedral is more convenient, then consider a short drive to the Japanese Friendship Garden at San Jose's Kelley Park, corner of Keyes and Senter roads. The park is a copy of the Korakuen Gardens in Okayama, Japan, and can be perfectly lovely in the spring, with flowering trees dropping delicate petals onto serene ponds where spectacular koi swim.

Dinner? Paolo's in San Jose (333 West San Carlos St., 408/294-2558), where the Italian emphasis on Easter takes a particularly tasty form.

Fourth of July

Two major choices are yours for this birthday of the United States. One would be a visit to Great America, the 100-acre, Americana-themed amusement park in Santa Clara (on Great America Parkway off the 101 Freeway; 408/988-1800). It's easy to spend an entire day here, riding the variety of roller coasters and other thrill rides and taking in the park's numerous entertainment shows. But don't fill up too much on the cotton candy and hot dogs. After your day at the park is done, there's an excellent American grill nearby—Birk's, 3955 Freedom Circle, adjacent to the red granite high-rise you see at Great America Parkway and 101. Dining here would be a perfect way to finish off your all-American day.

Option two is to take in the San Jose America Festival, centered around the city's downtown Guadalupe River Park, near West San Carlos Street and Almaden Boulevard—a multi-day celebration of free family entertainment stressing the region's multi-ethnic citizenry. It's a great way to observe the American melting pot—or tapestry of cultures, if you prefer—in action. And the celebration's numerous food booths offer you ample sustenance from most of the cultures represented. Information: 408/279-1775.

Both choices also offer that all-American favorite—fireworks—on the night of the Fourth, with major displays at both Great America and near the Children's Discovery Museum in downtown San Jose shortly after dark.

And, if you're especially adventuresome—and have plenty of stamina—take in a little bit of each of these celebratory events. Great America and downtown San Jose are linked by Santa Clara County Transit's light-rail line; it's roughly a half-hour trolley ride between the two.

Labor Day

You'll want to focus on labor, of course, and how Silicon Valley spends much of its work-time is on exhibit at The Tech Museum of Innovation, 145 West San Carlos St. across from the San Jose McEnery Convention Center. It's primarily designed to pique the scientific/technological interest of students from junior high on up, but that "on up" part guarantees that most of the displays also can keep adults interested for hours on end. The hands-on emphasis of The Tech means visitors can work with robotic arms, experience a semiconductor manufacturer's "clean room," use computers to design bicycles and earthquake-resistant buildings, chart their DNA, direct a simulated overflight of Mars and many of the other highly technical and highly fascinating aspects of work in Silicon Valley.

Then step outside and head for Tapestry in Talent, a multi-cultural, weekend-long arts festival centered along Park Avenue directly behind The Tech. Open 10 a.m. to dusk, it features performing, visual, culinary and literary arts displays and performances, and can be a great spot to shop for handmade gifts to take home with you.

If the festival is too wearing, drive south on Almaden Boulevard roughly 10 miles (the street's name will change to Almaden Expressway and then to Almaden Road, but keep the word Almaden foremost and you'll be OK.) At 21785 Almaden Rd. is Almaden Quicksilver Park, which offers you a glimpse of what labor was like in the earlier days of the valley, when miners sweated to extract mercury ore from mines in the area.

Cap off your excursion with dinner at La Foret restaurant in the adjacent village of New Almaden (21747 Bertram Rd; 408/997-3458). All that looking at work and thinking about labor must have made you hungry, and this charming restaurant overlooking Almaden Creek is a good choice for restoring your energy.

Thanksgiving

Few and far between are the restaurants that won't offer turkey dinner in some fashion this day, be it turkey en croute in a fancier continental eatery or turkey enchiladas in a homey

Mexican taqueria. The choice is up to you and your adventuresome palate.

But the day after Thanksgiving is one of the busiest shopping days of the year. If fortifying yourself with turkey has given you the strength for serious shopping, consider these places to visit:

Stanford Shopping Center, El Camino Real and Quarry Rd., Palo Alto; 415/328-0886. It's the most upscale of the upscale centers; bring money.

Valley Fair Shopping Center, Stevens Creek Blvd. at I-880, San Jose; 408/248-4451. The biggest of the valley's malls, offering the widest selection of stores—and the largest crowds of shoppers.

If it's discount bargains you're after, drive south to the **Pacific West Outlet Center** in Gilroy, Leavesley Road exit off Highway 101; 408/847-4155. This is the region's largest agglomeration of manufacturer and designer outlets, but also busy, and a favorite of some tour bus companies.

Or look for out-of-the-ordinary gifts at the annual **Harvest Festival** in the San Jose McEnery Convention Center, West San Carlos St. between Market Street and Almaden Boulevard; 408/778-6300. It's the valley's largest annual crafts festival featuring artisans in 19th Century costumes and continuous live entertainment. For a lower-key environment of arts and crafts shopping, there's the annual **San Jose State University Holiday Faire** at the SJS Student Union on campus near downtown San Jose; 408/924-6314.

Then when you're through, head for San Jose's **Japantown** (Jackson and Taylor streets between North First and North Seventh streets) for some soup at, say, Katana-Ya Ramen (154 East Jackson St., 408/286-3382), or sushi at Minato, (617 North Sixth St., 408/998-9711). You've more than likely had enough turkey for the week, and this should make you properly thankful for the change.

22
The Top 50 Companies

Silicon Valley is synonymous with business and industry, an international center with a distinctly high-tech flavor. But what makes the region truly unique at this particular point in its history is the availability of its founders and leaders, most of whom who are still living and working in the revolutionary field they helped create. Compare it, if you will, to Detroit in the early part of the 20th Century when the auto industry was beginning to change the face of America. It's as if Henry Ford, Walter Chrysler, Horace Dodge and their cohorts were on the job and at the height of their powers. In Silicon Valley, their counterparts ARE on the job, only their names are Gordon Moore and Andy Grove (Intel), Dean Watkins and Richard Johnson (Watkins-Johnson), John Warnock and Chuck Geschke (Adobe Systems), Jim Treybig (Tandem), Winston Chen (Solectron), T.J. Rodgers (Cypress Semiconductor), Scott McNealy (Sun Microsystems), Philippe Kahn (Borland International), Jim McCoy (Maxtor), Jim Morgan (Applied Materials), Gordon Campbell (Chips & Technologies), Jerry Sanders (Advanced Micro Devices), Al Shugart (Seagate), Finis Conner (Conner Peripherals), Robert Cohen and Peter Olson (Octel) and more whose names will become famous as their newer companies flourish. Even Bill Hewlett and David Packard still are around (although they leave the day-to-day running of Hewlett-

Packard largely to others), as well as Gene Amdahl (with Andor now—not the company that bears his name—a not unusual happening in this volatile business environment) and Steve Jobs and Steve Wozniak (the co-founders of Apple, each also now with other companies, Jobs with Next Inc. and Wozniak with Unison).

You may find yourself driving next to them on the freeway or rubbing elbows at a trade show or concert. And if you had been here only a few years earlier you might have met William Shockley, whose transistors set up the technological revolution, and Robert Noyce, whose integrated circuits threw everything into high gear. Silicon Valley is that new, in terms of both history and participants, and still is in evolution. This makes it a fascinating place to watch—or to do—business.

To assist you with that, here are the valley's top 50 publicly held companies, ranked by gross corporate revenue for the 1992 calendar year and excluding local divisions of national or international firms. (Note: Silicon Valley's largest employer, Lockheed Missiles & Space Co., is not included because it is a division of the larger Lockheed corporation, which is based elsewhere, as is technology industry giant IBM, also a major Silicon Valley player.)

1. **Hewlett-Packard Co.**, 3000 Hanover St., Palo Alto. Tel: 415/857-1501. Revenue: $17.1 billion. The company makes computing and electronic measuring equipment for business, industry, science, engineering, health care and education. Its more than 12,000 information products include computers and peripheral products, test and measuring instruments and computerized test systems, networking products, electronic components, hand-held calculators, medical electronic equipment, and instruments and systems for chemical analysis. The company employs approximately 93,000 people, with

plants in 26 U.S. cities, Europe, Japan, Latin America, Canada and the Asia Pacific region.

2. **Apple Computer Inc.,** 20525 Mariani Ave., Cupertino. Tel: 408/996-1010. Revenue: $7.2 billion. The company develops, manufactures and markets personal computer systems for business, education, science, engineering and government. Included in the systems are printers, monitors, scanners, and system software for networking products. The company employs approximately 15,000 persons in the United States, Europe, Canada, Australia, Japan and Singapore.

3. **Intel Corp.,** 3085 Bowers Ave., Santa Clara. Tel: 408/765-8080. Revenue: $5.8 billion. A pioneer in the development of complex integrated circuits and the innovator of the first microprocessor, the firm today is a leading supplier of microcomputer components, modules and systems. It employs approximately 25,800 persons worldwide.

4. **Consolidated Freightways,** P.O. Box 10340, Palo Alto. Tel: 415/494-2900. Revenue: $4.01 billion. The company is a diversified freight transportation company with operations throughout North America and 88 foreign countries, employing approximately 37,900 persons. Principal subsidiaries are: CF Motor Freight, a North American long-haul carrier; Con-Way Transportation Services, a regional next-day trucking and intermodal services company; Emery Worldwide, a North American and international air freight carrier; and Menlo Logistics, a transportation logistics management business. The company also has customs brokerage, equipment supply and trailer manufacturing businesses.

5. **Sun Microsystems Inc.,** 2550 Garcia Ave., Mountain View.

Tel: 415/960-1300. Revenue: $3.6 billion. The company, through its subsidiaries, is a leading manufacturer of systems for client/server computing: workstations, servers, system software, printers, networking products and related products that use the UNIX operating system. It has manufacturing facilities in Milpitas, Westford, Mass., and Scotland, an engineering center in France, a development center in Canada, a logistics center in Germany and joint engineering/distribution agreements for Japan, employing approximately 12,800 persons.

6. **Seagate Technology Inc.**, 920 Disc Dr., Scotts Valley. Tel: 408/438-6550. Revenue: $3.1 billion. The company is an independent designer, manufacturer and marketer of disk storage products for the computer systems industry, principally rigid magnetic disk drives for notebook, laptop and portable computers, personal computers and technical workstations, mainframes and supercomputers. It employs approximately 40,000 persons and has manufacturing facilities in the United States and abroad, plus sales offices worldwide.

7. **Amdahl Corp.**, 1250 East Arques Ave., Sunnyvale. Tel: 408/746-6000. Revenue: $2.5 billion. The company designs, develops, manufactures, markets and services large-scale, high-performance data processing systems, including general-purpose mainframe computers, data storage subsystems, data communications products and software. It also provides education and consulting services. There are approximately 8,800 Amdahl employees worldwide, and some 120 sales offices serving customers in more than 25 countries.

8. **Conner Peripherals Inc.**, 3081 Zanker Rd., San Jose. Tel:

408/456-4500. Revenue: $2.2 billion. Conner sells, designs and builds a complete line of Winchester disk drives for a wide range of computer applications, including network servers and workstations, desktop, laptop and notebook computers, and sub-notebook, pen-based and palm-top systems. Its approximately 11,500 employees work in manufacturing operations in the United States, Malaysia, Italy and Scotland; in research and development facilities in California and Colorado; and in sales and service offices throughout the U.S., Asia and Europe.

9. **Tandem Computers Inc.**, 19333 Vallco Parkway, Cupertino. Tel: 408/725-6000. Revenue: $2.1 billion. Tandem is a leading supplier of on-line transaction processing systems and networks for critical information processing requirements. It is the first company to offer fault-tolerant systems designed to operate continuously despite component failures. The company and its subsidiaries employ approximately 10,500 persons in more than 180 locations worldwide.

10. **Syntex Corp.**, 3401 Hillview Ave., Palo Alto. Tel: 415/855-5050. Revenue: $2 billion. An international health-care company, it develops, manufactures and markets human and animal pharmaceutical products and medical diagnostic systems. It has approximately 11,000 employees, slightly more than half of them working in the United States and the remainder in Canada, Europe, Japan, Mexico and the United Kingdom.

11. **National Semiconductor Corp.**, 2900 Semiconductor Dr., Santa Clara. Tel: 408/721-5000. Revenue: $1.9 billion. National Semi is a leading developer, manufacturer and distributor of semiconductors and related products, aimed at analog-

intensive markets, communications markets and markets for personal systems. It employs approximately 26,200 persons at facilities across the United States, Europe, Asia and the Middle East.

12. **Quantum Corp.**, 500 McCarthy Blvd., Milpitas. Tel: 408/894-4000. Revenue: $1.54 billion. Quantum designs, manufactures and markets high-performance, small form-factor hard disk drives for use in personal computers, desktop workstations and notebook systems. It sells its products directly to original equipment manufacturers, through distributors to systems integrators, value-added resellers and smaller original equipment manufacturers, and through dealers and retail outlets to end users. Its approximately 2,200 employees work in the United States, Asia and Europe.

13. **Advanced Micro Devices Inc.**, 901 Thompson Pl., Sunnyvale. Tel: 408/732-2400. Revenue: $1.51 billion. The company designs and manufactures integrated circuits, specializing in microprocessors and related peripherals, memories, programmable logic devices and circuits for telecommunications, office automation and networking applications, for manufacturers of equipment for personal and networked computation and communication. It employs approximately 11,500 persons worldwide.

14. **Raychem Corp.**, 300 Constitution Dr., Menlo Park. Tel: 415/361-3333. Revenue: $1.36 billion. The company designs, manufactures and markets materials science products based on physical properties of plastics, metals and chemicals; wiring and cable products and heat-shrinkable tubing for transportation and aerospace; heat-shrinkable tubing for gas and water utilities and pipelines; circuit-protection devices for electrical power and consumer electronics products; splice

closures and fiber optics technology for telecommunications; self-regulating heaters for commercial and residential buildings; and leak-detection systems for environmental protection. It employs approximately 11,000 people, roughly half of them in the United States and the remainder in more than 40 other countries.

15. **Varian Associates Inc.**, 3100 Hansen Way, Palo Alto. Tel: 415/493-4000. Revenue: $1.28 billion. The company designs, manufactures and markets a diverse line of technology products including: microwave, power and special-purpose electron tubes and devices for communications, industry, defense and research; analytical instruments for science and industry; wafer fabrication equipment for the semiconductor industry; radiation systems for cancer therapy and non-destructive testing; and vacuum equipment and leak detectors for industrial and scientific processes. It employs approximately 8,000 persons in the United States, Asia and Europe.

16. **Maxtor Corp.** 211 River Oaks Parkway, San Jose. Tel: 408/432-1700. Revenue: $1.04 billion. A wide range of mass storage products are Maxtor's principal products, including Winchester disk drives and optical drives for personal computers, portable computers, workstations, local area networks, CAD/CAM systems, artificial intelligence systems, minicomputers and mainframe computers. It employs approximately 9,000 persons at manufacturing facilities in the United States and Asia and at sales, administrative and service facilities worldwide.

17. **Silicon Graphics Inc.**, 2011 North Shoreline Blvd., Mountain View. Tel: 415/960-1980. Revenue: $949.2 million. Silicon Graphics is a leading developer and supplier of visual computing systems, pioneering three-dimensional

computing and offering a wide range of graphics technology workstations and servers for corporate computing environments. It has manufacturing facilities in California, Switzerland and Japan, and support and sales offices worldwide, employing approximately 3,500 persons.

18. **Applied Materials Inc.**, 3050 Bowers Ave., Santa Clara. Tel: 408/748-5227. Revenue: $799.96 million. The company is the leading independent producer of wafer fabrication systems for the semiconductor industry, particularly epitaxial deposition systems, plasma etch systems and chemical vapor deposition (CVD) systems, including tungsten CVD. It employs approximately 3,900 persons worldwide.

19. **Adia Services Inc.**, 64 Willow Place, Menlo Park. Tel: 415/324-0696. Revenue: $742.7 million. Adia is a major supplier of temporary and full-time personnel in a variety of skill areas, including secretarial, clerical, light industrial, accounting, data processing, word processing, health care, technical, and banking and financial services. It employs approximately 1,900 persons nationwide, maintaining 558 offices in the United States and more than 1,400 offices worldwide.

20. **LSI Logic Corp.**, 1551 McCarthy Blvd., Milpitas. Tel: 408/433-8000. Revenue: $617 million. The company is a leading designer and manufacturer of application-specific integrated circuits, with products including those for reduced instruction-set computer microprocessors, digital signal processing, video compressions, chipsets and graphics. It employs approximately 3,300 persons worldwide.

21. **Anthem Electronics Inc.**, 1160 Ridder Park Dr., San Jose. Tel: 408/453-1200. Revenue: $538.4 million. The company distributes semiconductor and subsystem products, including

disk and tape drives, and through a subsidiary manufactures and markets computer connectivity products. It maintains distribution centers nationwide and in Europe, and employs approximately 675 persons.

22. **Solectron Corp.**, 847 Gibraltar Dr., Milpitas. Tel: 408/957-8500. Revenue: $531.2 million. The company supplies customized, integrated manufacturing services to original equipment manufacturers in the electronics industry, with primary emphasis on surface-mount interconnection technologies. It employs approximately 3,500 persons at manufacturing facilities at Milpitas and Malaysia.

23. **3Com Corp.** 5400 Bayfront Plaza, Santa Clara. Tel: 408/764-5000. Revenue: $502.2 million. 3Com is a leading independent global data networking company, providing multivendor connectivity for organizations and businesses worldwide. It designs, manufactures, markets and supports a wide range of networking systems based on industry standards and open systems architecture. Approximately 1,900 persons are in its employ.

24. **Cisco Systems Inc.**, 1525 O'Brien Dr., Menlo Park. Tel: 415/326-1941. Revenue: $473.5 million. Cisco is a leading supplier of high-performance multimedia and multiprotocol internetworking products, such as routers, bridges, terminal servers and network management products. It maintains operations in the United States, Canada, England, France and Sweden, employing approximately 875 persons.

25. **Borland International Inc.**, 1800 Green Hills Rd., Scotts Valley. Tel: 408/438-8400. Revenue: $464 million. The company is a leading developer and marketer of business application software and programming languages, as well as

personal computer and database software. It employs approximately 1,900 persons at manufacturing facilities in the United States and Ireland and at sales offices and subsidiaries in the U.S., Asia/Pacific and Europe.

26. **Read-Rite Corp.**, 345 Los Coches St., Milpitas. Tel: 408/957-2156. Revenue: $461 million. Read-Rite designs, manufactures and markets thin-film components that record and retrieve information from the surface of disks in computer disk drives. It employs approximately 1,900 persons at facilities in California, Malaysia, Thailand and Japan.

27. **The Ask Group,** 2440 El Camino Real, Mountain View. Tel: 415/969-4442. Revenue: $447.8 million. Ask and its subsidiaries comprise one of the 10 largest software companies in the world with nearly 100 sales offices on four continents and more than 2,000 employees worldwide. Its products include database and application development tools and software for manufacturing and financial management applications.

28. **Cadence Design Systems Inc.**, 555 River Oaks Parkway, San Jose. Tel: 408/943-1234. Revenue: $434.5 million. The company develops and markets electronic design automation software products and services. Its approximately 2,500 employees work at division offices throughout the United States, at research and development centers in the U.S., India, Taiwan and the United Kingdom, and at sales offices in North America, Europe and Asia/Pacific.

29. **VLSI Technology Inc.**, 1109 McKay Dr., San Jose. Tel: 408/434-3000. Revenue: $428.5 million. VLSI manufactures complex application-specific integrated circuits and application-specific standard products, and, through a subsidiary,

develops and markets computer-aided engineering software for advanced integrated-circuit design. It employs approximately 2,400 persons, has manufacturing facilities in San Jose, Texas and Arizona, and also maintains offices elsewhere in North America, Europe, Asia/Pacific and Japan.

30. **SynOptics Inc.**, 4401 Great America Parkway, Santa Clara. Tel: 408/988-2400. Revenue: $388.8 million. The company supplies managing and processing systems for local area network computer uses, selling its products to original equipment manufacturers, systems integrators, distributors, resellers and end users. It has approximately 1,200 employees in 42 offices worldwide.

31. **Acuson Corp.**, 1220 Charleston Rd., Mountain View. Tel: 415/969-9112. Revenue: $342.8 million. Acuson designs, manufactures and markets premium quality medical diagnostic ultrasound imaging systems, selling its products primarily to hospitals and clinics for use in obstetrical, abdominal, urological, vascular and cardiac applications. It employs approximately 1,700 people worldwide, manufacturing its products at Mountain View and maintaining sales and service offices in North America, Europe and Asia/Pacific.

32. **Komag Inc.**, 275 South Hillview Dr., Milpitas. Tel: 408/246-2300. Revenue: $326.8 million. Komag is a leader in material science technology and the world's largest manufacturer of thin-film disks used in high performance Winchester disk drives. Its operations, employing approximately 3,100 people, are located in the United States, Japan and Malaysia.

33. **Inmac Corp.**, 2465 Augustine Dr., Santa Clara. Tel: 408/727-1970. Revenue: $312.9 million. Inmac is a catalog

marketer of data communications products and computer accessories, furniture, data storage media and supplies in the United States and Europe. The company employs approximately 1,300 persons servicing a mailing list of more than 2 million, and manufactures its own cable and data communications peripherals in San Jose.

34. Diasonics Corp., 1565 Barber Lane, Milpitas. Tel: 408/432-9000. Revenue: $299.5 million. The company develops, makes and markets computer-based imaging systems for hospitals, clinics and private practice. Its primary products include ultrasound systems, specialty X-ray systems, urology systems, lithotripsy treatment products and surgical tables. It employs approximately 1,400 persons worldwide.

35. Informix Corp., 4100 Bohannon Dr., Menlo Park. Tel: 415/926-6300. Revenue: $283.6 million. Informix is a leading manufacturer of UNIX-based database management systems and software. It employs approximately 1,400 persons in Silicon Valley and abroad.

36. Cirrus Logic Inc., 1300 West Warren Ave., Fremont. Tel: 510/623-8300. Revenue: $282.8 million. Fast-growing Cirrus manufactures integrated circuits and software for control functions of computer peripherals. Approximately 1,200 persons are in its employ worldwide.

37. Adaptec Inc., 691 South Milpitas Blvd., Milpitas. Tel: 408/945-8600. Revenue: $274.3 million. Adaptec specializes in the manufacture of input-output components used by microcomputers and peripherals. It employs approximately 1.400 people worldwide.

38. Cypress Semiconductor Corp., 3901 North First St., San

Jose. Tel: 408/943-2600. Revenue: $272.2 million. The company produces high performance integrated circuits for niche markets, principally high-performance computers, telecommunications, instrumentation and military systems. It employs approximately 1,500 people in North America, Europe and Asia/Pacific.

39. **Adobe Systems Inc.**, 1585 Charleston Rd., Mountain View. Tel: 415/961-4400. Revenue: $266 million. Adobe develops, markets and supports computer software products and technologies that create, display, print and communicate electronic documents. It also licenses its technology to major computer and publishing suppliers and markets a line of type and application software products. It has approximately 850 employees worldwide.

40. **Watkins-Johnson Co.**, 3333 Hillview Ave., Palo Alto. Tel: 415/493-4141. Revenue: $264.4 million. The company specializes in defense-electronics products, semiconductor manufacturing equipment and environmental consulting services. It employs approximately 2,500 persons at manufacturing plants in California, Maryland and England, and in sales and service offices there and in Colorado.

41. **Measurex Corp.**, 1 Results Way, Cupertino. Tel: 408/255-1500. Revenue: $252.6 million. Measurex supplies computer-integrated control and information systems for manufacturing processes, both continuous and batch, principally in the pulp and paper, metals, rubber and chemicals industries. It employs approximately 2,300 persons in 39 offices and plants in 25 countries worldwide.

42. **Alza Corp.**, 950 Page Mill Rd., Palo Alto. Tel: 415/494-5000. Revenue: $250.5 million. Alza is a leading developer

and manufacturer of therapeutic drug delivery systems. It employs approximately 1,300 persons worldwide.

43. California Microwave Inc., 985 Almanor Ave., Sunnyvale. Tel: 408/732-4000. Revenue: $226.7 million. The company is a leading supplier of satellite earth stations and equipment for international voice, video and data circuits. Its wireless products support data transmission, broadcasting, government, mobile and cellular operations, as well as personal communications systems. It employs approximately 1,300 persons, and operates manufacturing facilities in Arizona, California, Florida, Maryland, Massachusetts and New York.

44. Robert Half International Inc., 2884 Sand Hill Rd., Menlo Park. Tel: 415/854-9700. Revenue: $220.2 million. The company claims to be the world's first and largest personnel service company specializing in the fields of accounting, finance, information systems and banking. Its Robert Half division places workers in permanent jobs in those fields; its Accountemps division places workers in temporary positions. It employs approximately 900 persons, and maintains more than 150 offices worldwide.

45. Logitech, 6505 Kaiser Dr., Fremont. Tel: 510/795-8500. Revenue: $218.8 million. Logitech is a leading developer and manufacturer of computer pointing devices, such as mouse and track-ball systems. Approximately 1,800 persons are in its employ.

46. Symantec Corp., 10201 Torre Ave., Cupertino. Tel: 408/253-9600. Revenue: $217.8 million. Symantec develops, manufactures and markets software for stand-alone and networked personal computers, as well as productivity applications and development languages and tools. It employs approximately 1,000 persons in 35 locations worldwide, including North and South America, Europe and Australia.

47. **Coherent Inc.**, 5100 Patrick Henry Dr., Santa Clara. Tel: 408/764-400. Revenue: $211 million. Coherent designs, manufactures and maintains more than 1,000 different laser products for science, medicine and industry. It, and its subsidiaries, employ approximately 1,300 persons in offices in the United States, Europe and Asia.

48. **Octel Communications Corp.**, 890 Tasman Dr., Milpitas. Tel: 408/321-6500. Revenue: $210.7 million. Octel designs, makes and markets voice information processing servers and software, systems allowing callers to access multiple information sources (voice, image and data) by touch-tone telephone. It employs approximately 1,600 persons.

49. **Silicon Valley Group Inc.**, 2240 Ringwood Dr., San Jose. Tel: 408/434-0500. Revenue: $202.9 million. The company designs, manufactures and markets equipment used in the primary stages of semiconductor manufacturing, including track systems for photoresist processing, thermal processing systems and photolithography exposure systems. It employs approximately 1,400 persons worldwide, the bulk at manufacturing facilities in California and Connecticut.

50. **Integrated Device Technology Inc.**, 2975 Stender Way, Santa Clara. Tel: 408/727-6116. Revenue: $202.7 million. The company designs and manufactures complex proprietary and industry-standard integrated circuits using high-performance complementary metal oxide semiconductor (CMOS) and bipolar CMOS (BICMOS) technology. It employs approximately 2,300 persons in facilities worldwide.

23
Venture Capitalists

Many people have started businesses in Silicon Valley. Many others come to Silicon Valley to start businesses. Either way, they often seek the assistance of venture capitalists — those with money to invest (often people who already have made their fortunes in earlier businesses) in these new ventures. It's a specialized field, and Silicon Valley — particularly Sand Hill Road where it separates Palo Alto and Menlo Park — boasts one of the nation's largest concentrations.

A sampling of the leading venture capital firms, should you be so inclined:

Bay Partners, 10600 North De Anza Blvd., Suite 100, Cupertino. Tel: 408/725-2444.

Harvest Ventures, 19200 Stevens Creek Blvd., Suite 220, Cupertino. Tel: 408/996-3200.

Institutional Venture Partners, 3000 Sand Hill Rd., Building 2, Suite 290, Menlo Park. Tel: 415/854-0132.

InterWest Partners, 3000 Sand Hill Rd., Building 3, Suite 255, Menlo Park. Tel: 415/854-8585.

Kleiner Perkins Caufield & Byers, 2200 Geng Rd., Suite 205, Palo Alto. Tel: 415/424-1660.

Mayfield Fund, 2200 Sand Hill Rd., Menlo Park. Tel: 415/854-5560.

McCown DeLeeuw & Co., 3000 Sand Hill Rd., Building 3,

Suite 290, Menlo Park. Tel: 415/854-6000.

Mohr, Davidow Ventures, 3000 Sand Hill Rd., Building 1, Suite 240, Menlo Park. Tel: 415/854-7236.

New Enterprise Associates, 3000 Sand Hill Rd., Building 4, Suite 235, Menlo Park. Tel: 415/854-2660.

Sequoia Capital, 3000 Sand Hill Rd., Building 4, Suite 280, Menlo Park. Tel: 415/854-3927.

U.S. Venture Partners, 2180 Sand Hill Rd., Suite 300, Menlo Park. Tel: 415/854-9080.

Handy Telephone Numbers

Emergency

Police 911
Fire 911
Ambulance 911
Crisis Intervention 408/299-6234
Poison Control 408/299-5112
Suicide Prevention (Central County) 408/279-3312
       (South County) 408/683-2482

Medical Referrals

Dental 408/289-1480
Physician 408/998-5700
Handicapped assistance 800/400-6222

Road Conditions

California Highway Patrol 408/436-1404

Time
408/767-8900

Telephone Directory Assistance
411

Weather
415/364-7974

Visitor Information

Information Center 408/283-8833
Special Events Hotline 408/295-2265
Convention/Visitors Bureau 408/295-9600